Afterschool MATH CLUB Achievers

Patsy F. Kanter

Alanna Arenivas

Shara S. Hammet

Barbara B. Irvin

Leigh E. Palmer

Annette Raphel

Kimberly M. Tolbert

GReaT SoURCe

EDUCATION GROUP

A Houghton Mifflin Company

New Ways to Know

Credits

Editorial: Kathy Kellman, Pearl Ling & Associates, Susan Rogalski

Design/Production: Taurins Design, NYC

Creative Art: Scot Ritchie

Technical Art: Taurins Design, NYC

2, 4, 6, 8 Pattern Puzzler

Today's Challenge

1. Connect the dots in order by counting by twos starting with 2.

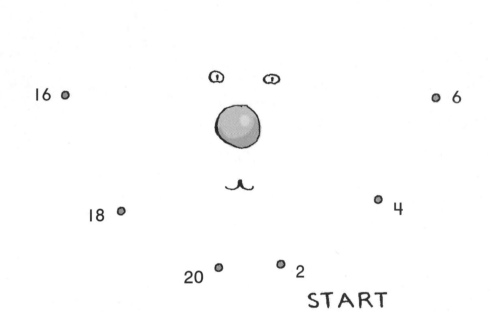

START

Go Further

2. List all the numbers that you connected to make the figure above.

   <u> 2 </u>, ____, ____, ____, ____, ____, ____, ____, ____, ____

3. Look at the list of numbers above. Tell a friend about the pattern you see.

On today's activity: (Circle one) I did great! I did OK. I need help.

Name   **Date**   1

Today's Challenge — Draw a line to match the correct letter.

1. Name one way to show 13.

A.

2. Name one way to show 21.

B. |||| |||| |||| |||| |

3. Name one way to show 6.

C.

4. Name one way to show 16.

D.

5. Name one way to show 18.

E.

6. Name one way to show 7.

F.

7. Name one way to show 12.

G.

Go Further

8. Draw a picture to show the number 16 .

On today's activity: (Circle one) ➧ I did great! ➧ I did OK. ➧ I need help.

Date

Today's Challenge — For questions 1 and 2, circle Yes or No.

1. **Clues:**

   a. Does it roll?   Yes   No

   b. Can it be stacked?   Yes   No

   c. Can it slide?   Yes   No

   d. Does it have a round base?   Yes   No

   What is my name? _____

2. **Clues:**

   a. Can it be stacked?   Yes   No

   b. Does it have a round base?   Yes   No

   c. Can it slide?   Yes   No

   d. Does it roll?   Yes   No

   What is my name? _____

Go Further

3. Solve this riddle.

   Clues:

   · I have 6 faces that are exactly the same.

   · I can slide, but not roll.

   · I can be stacked.

   · My nickname is "boxy."

   · What is my name? _____

4. Write your own riddle for a friend to solve.

   Clues: _____

   _____

   What is my name? _____   Friend's name _____

On today's activity: (Circle one)   I did great!   I did OK.   I need help.

Name _____   **Date** _____   3

Today's Challenge Look for pairs of numbers with sums that equal 6 or 7. Write the facts in the table.

4	3	5	6
0	3	1	6
6	2	5	7
5	4	2	0

Sums that equal 6	Sums that equal 7
_____ + _____	_____ + _____
_____ + _____	_____ + _____
_____ + _____	_____ + _____
_____ + _____	_____ + _____

Go Further Create your own Math Jumble. Include at least five pairs of numbers with sums that equal 6 or 7. Have a friend write five facts with sums that equal 6 or 7.

_____

_____

_____

_____

_____

Friend's name _____

On today's activity: (Circle one) I did great! I did OK. I need help.

4 Name

Date

Get Started — Rule out two. Write why. Fill in the correct circle.

Which of the following expressions is equal to 20?

(A) 30 − 5 _____   (B) 11 + 9 _____

(C) 1 dime _____   (D) 10 + 5 _____

Today's Challenge

1. Which of the following expressions is equal to 25?

(A) 20 + 20 _____ ☐

(B) 10 + 15 _____ ☐

(C) 50 − 10 _____ ☐

(D) 1 quarter + 1 nickel _____ ☐

2. Which of the following expressions is not equal to 15?

(A) 10 + 5 _____ ☐

(B) 3 nickels _____ ☐

(C) 20 − 5 _____ ☐

(D) 10 + 10 _____ ☐

Total points for Today's Challenge: _____

On today's activity: (Circle one) — I did great! — I did OK. — I need help.

Name _____   Date _____   5

2, 4, 6, 8 Pattern Puzzler

Today's Challenge — Color the blocks as shown. Use what you know to continue each pattern.

1.

red	yellow	yellow	red	yellow	yellow			

2.

blue	orange	orange	blue	orange	orange			

3.

yellow	green	green	yellow	green	green			

Go Further — Color the blocks as shown. Use what you know to fill in the missing colors in the pattern.

4.

blue	yellow	yellow	blue	yellow		blue		yellow

5.

orange	green	green		green	green	orange		green

6.

red		blue	red	blue	blue	red	blue	

On today's activity: (Circle one) — I did great! — I did OK. — I need help.

6 **Name**

Date

Today's Challenge — Choose answers from the box to fill in the blanks.

1 foot	6 inches	3000 feet	1 inch
3 feet	1 yard	2 feet	200 miles

1. The special name for 3 feet is _____.

2. The distance between 2 cities can be _____.

3. The special name for 12 inches is _____.

4. The sum of 1 foot + 1 foot is _____.

5. The height of a mountain can be _____.

6. The length of half a foot is _____.

7. The length of an inchworm is _____.

8. The length that equals 1 yard is _____.

Go Further

9. Make a list of some tools you can use to measure with if you do not have a ruler.

_____

_____

_____

On today's activity: (Circle one) — I did great! — I did OK. — I need help.

Name   **Date**   7

Game Time

Game Time

Week 2•Activity 8

Today's Challenge ⟍ **For questions 1 and 2, circle Yes or No.**

1. **Clues:**

   a. Does it have straight sides?   Yes   No

   b. Can you use it to measure the length of your finger?   Yes   No

   c. Can you blow air into it?   Yes   No

   What is my name? _____

2. **Clues:**

   a. Does it have straight sides?   Yes   No

   b. Can you use it to measure the length of your finger?   Yes   No

   c. Can you use it to find the length of a window?   Yes   No

   What is my name? _____

Go Further ⟍ Scavenger Hunt

3. Find 5 objects in the classroom to measure. Use the length of your finger or the length of your arm to measure the objects.

Object	Length
_____	_____
_____	_____
_____	_____
_____	_____
_____	_____

On today's activity: (Circle one) ⟍ I did great! ⟍ I did OK. ⟍ I need help.

8   Name _____

Date _____

Today's Challenge Look for pairs of numbers with sums of 7 or 8. Write the facts in the table.

2	5	0	8
6	1	7	3
3	4	2	5
5	3	4	4

Sums of 7	Sums of 8
_____ + _____	_____ + _____
_____ + _____	_____ + _____
_____ + _____	_____ + _____
_____ + _____	_____ + _____

Go Further Create your own Math Jumble. Include at least five pairs of numbers with sums of 7 or 8. Have a friend write five facts with sums of 7 or 8.

_____

_____

_____

_____

_____

Friend's name _____

On today's activity: (Circle one) I did great! I did OK. I need help.

Name **Date** 9

Get Started — Rule out two. Write why. Fill in the correct circle.

Morris spent 10¢ in the gumball machine. His brother also spent 10¢. Which addition expression shows how much they spent altogether?

(A) 10¢ − 10¢ _____   **(B)** 10¢ − 2¢ _____

(C) 10¢ + 10¢ _____   **(D)** 2¢ + 2¢ _____

Today's Challenge

1. Elsie sells 4 tickets to the school play today. Marc sells the same number of tickets. Which addition expression shows how many tickets they sell altogether?

(A) 4 + 4 _____

(B) 8 − 4 _____

(C) 4 − 1 _____

(D) 4 − 4 _____

2. Anna has 8 stamps. She buys 8 more at the post office. Which addition expression shows how many stamps she has altogether?

(A) 8 + 10 _____

(B) 8 + 8 _____

(C) 8 + 2 _____

(D) 8 − 8 _____

Total points for Today's Challenge: _____

On today's activity: (Circle one) — I did great! — I did OK. — I need help.

10 Name

Date

2, 4, 6, 8 Pattern Puzzler

Today's Challenge Continue each pattern by drawing the next two shapes.

1.  _____ _____

2. _____ _____

3.  _____ _____

Go Further Draw the missing shape for each pattern.

4.  _____

5.  _____

6.

On today's activity: (Circle one) I did great! I did OK. I need help.

Name

Date

11

Today's Challenge — Choose a number from the box to fill in the blanks.

3	7	3 and 5	0
6	5	8	4

1. The sum of 4 + 2 is _____.

2. The number you add to 3 to get a sum of 8 is _____.

3. The numbers between 2 and 6 that add up to 8 are _____.

4. The number I add to 0 to get a sum of 8 is _____.

5. The number I add to 2 to get a sum of 6 is _____.

6. The number you add to 5 to get a sum of 8 is _____.

7. The sum of 1 + 6 is _____.

8. The number I add to 7 to get a sum of 7 is _____.

Go Further

9. Write 3 different ways to show a sum of 8.

_____

_____

_____

On today's activity: (Circle one) — I did great! — I did OK. — I need help.

Name

Date

Today's Challenge — For questions 1 and 2, circle Yes or No.

1. **Clues:**

   a. Is it round?   Yes   No

   b. Does it roll?   Yes   No

   c. Can it be stacked?   Yes   No

   d. Does it have a square face?   Yes   No

   What is my name? _____

2. **Clues:**

   a. Does it look like a soup can?   Yes   No

   b. Does it have 2 round faces?   Yes   No

   c. Can it be stacked?   Yes   No

   d. Does it roll?   Yes   No

   What is my name? _____

Go Further

3. Solve this riddle.

   Clues:

   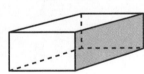

   · I have 6 rectangular faces.

   · I have 12 edges.

   · I look like a cereal box.

   · I am a _____ prism.

4. Write your own riddle for a friend to solve.

   Clues: _____

   _____

   I am a _____ Friend's name _____

On today's activity: (Circle one) — I did great! — I did OK. — I need help.

Name   **Date**

Today's Challenge Look for pairs of numbers with sums of 9. Write the facts in the table.

9	6	3	2
0	1	8	7
4	5	3	1
3	4	6	8

Sums of 9

_____ + _____

_____ + _____

_____ + _____

_____ + _____

Go Further Create your own Math Jumble. Include at least five pairs of numbers with sums of 9. Have a friend write five facts with sums of 9.

_____

_____

_____

_____

_____

Friend's name _____

On today's activity: (Circle one) I did great! I did OK. I need help.

14 Name

Date

Get Started

Rule out two. Write why. Fill in the correct circle.

George drew a shape that has only straight lines. Which of these did George draw?

(A) ⬤ _____   (B) ⬭ _____

(C) 🌙 _____   (D) ⬆ _____

Today's Challenge

1. Pick the shape without any curves.

(A) _____ ☐

(B) _____ ☐

(C) _____ ☐

(D) _____ ☐

2. Pick the shape with 10 straight lines.

(A) _____ ☐

(B) _____ ☐

(C) _____ ☐

(D) _____ ☐

Total points for Today's Challenge: _____

On today's activity: (Circle one) I did great! I did OK. I need help.

Name   Date   15

2, 4, 6, 8 Pattern Puzzler

Today's Challenge — Complete each set.

1. $3 - 1 =$ _____

$3 - 2 =$ _____

$3 - 3 =$ _____

2. $5 - 1 =$ _____

$5 - 2 =$ _____

$5 - 3 =$ _____

$5 - 4 =$ _____

$5 - 5 =$ _____

3. $6 - 1 =$ _____

$6 - 2 =$ _____

$6 - 3 =$ _____

$6 - 4 =$ _____

$6 - 5 =$ _____

$6 - 6 =$ _____

Go Further

4. Look at all the equations above. Which equations have an answer of 0? Write the equations in the blanks.

_____   _____   _____

5. What is the same about the equations you wrote in problem 4?

_____

_____

On today's activity: (Circle one) ▰ I did great! ▰ I did OK. ▰ I need help.

Name

Date

Today's Challenge — Choose a number from the box to fill in the blanks.

26	75	98	81	55
52	18	32	35	13

1. The first odd number after 80 is _____.

2. The even number between 25 and 27 is _____.

3. The even number closest to 30 is _____.

4. The second odd number after 10 is _____.

5. The odd number that is halfway between 70 and 80 is _____.

6. The largest even number less than 100 is _____.

7. The odd number with both digits the same is _____.

8. The even number closest to 50 is _____.

9. The odd number that is halfway between 30 and 40 is _____.

10. The even number that is between 16 and 20 is _____.

Go Further

11. Write all the odd numbers between 30 and 40.

_____

On today's activity: (Circle one) ◁ I did great! ◁ I did OK. ◁ I need help.

Name　　　　　　　　　　　　　　　　**Date**

Go Further — Follow the directions to cross out numbers.

1	16	12	5
8	2	6	11
9	15	7	10
4	14	13	3

- Cross out all numbers that you land on if you skip count by 5.
- Cross out all numbers that have 1 in the ones place.
- Cross out one more than a pair.
- Double 6. Cross out the number that is one more.
- Cross out 4 + 4.
- Cross out 4 + 4 + 1.
- Cross out numbers that you land on if you skip count by 2.

1. Which number is left? _____

2. Is the number 7 odd or even?

_____

Use words, pictures, or number sentences to show your thinking.

_____

_____

On today's activity: (Circle one) ✏ I did great! ✏ I did OK. ✏ I need help.

Today's Challenge — Look for pairs of numbers with sums of 10. Write the facts in the table.

2	8	9	1
7	6	5	5
3	4	5	7
4	6	7	3

Sums of 10

_____ + _____

_____ + _____

_____ + _____

_____ + _____

Go Further — Create your own Math Jumble. Include at least five pairs of numbers with sums of 10. Have a friend write five facts with sums of 10.

_____

_____

_____

_____

_____

Friend's name _____

On today's activity: (Circle one) — I did great! — I did OK. — I need help.

Name _____ **Date** _____

19

Get Started — Rule out two. Write why. Fill in the correct circle.

To paint the school library, you should buy paint that comes in which size container?

A cup _____   **B** pint _____

C quart _____   **D** gallon _____

Today's Challenge

1. Marvin buys milk during lunchtime at school. Which container does he buy?

A cup _____

B pint _____

C quart _____

D gallon _____

2. Mrs. Chan needs enough juice for her family for a whole week. Which size container should she buy?

A cup _____

B pint _____

C quart _____

D gallon _____

Total points for Today's Challenge: _____

On today's activity: (Circle one) — I did great! — I did OK. — I need help.

Today's Challenge Use markers or crayons to color the blocks shown. Then, finish each pattern by coloring the rest of the blocks to match the pattern.

1. | red | blue | red | blue | red | blue | | |

2. | yellow | red | red | yellow | red | red | yellow | | |

3. | green | blue | blue | green | blue | blue | | | |

Go Further Use markers or crayons to color the blocks shown. Use the pattern to help you find the missing colors.

4. | red | green | green | yellow | red | green | | yellow | |

On today's activity: (Circle one) I did great! I did OK. I need help.

Name **Date** 21

Today's Challenge
Choose a number from the box to fill in the blanks.

16	7	12	4	19
15	8	13	9	5

1. The sum of $5 + 5 + 5$ equals _____.

2. The sum of $1 + 1 + 1 + 1$ equals _____.

3. The sum of $15 + 4$ equals _____.

4. The sum of $7 + 0$ equals _____.

5. The sum of $8 + 8$ equals _____.

6. The sum of $3 + 3 + 3$ equals _____.

7. The sum of $0 + 5$ equals _____.

8. The sum of $6 + 7$ equals _____.

9. The sum of $2 + 2 + 2 + 2$ equals5 _____.

Go Further

10. Describe how you would use doubles to find the sum of $6 + 8$.

_____

_____

On today's activity: (Circle one) I did great! I did OK. I need help.

Date

Today's Challenge — **For questions 1 and 2, circle** Yes **or** No **for the solid shown.**

1. **Clues:**

   a. Does it roll?   Yes   No

   b. Can it be stacked?   Yes   No

   c. Can it slide?   Yes   No

   d. Are all the faces square?   Yes   No

   What is my name? _____

2. **Clues:**

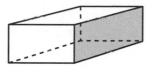

   a. Can it be stacked?   Yes   No

   b. Are all the faces rectangles?   Yes   No

   c. Can it slide?   Yes   No

   d. Does it roll?   Yes   No

   What is my name? _____

Go Further

3. Now it is your turn. Draw 2 real life items that are in the shape of a rectangular solid.

On today's activity: (Circle one) ✏ I did great! ✏ I did OK. ✏ I need help.

Today's Challenge ✎ Look for strings of numbers that can be used to write addition facts that have 0 or 1 as an addend. Write the facts.

4	1	3	9
8	5	4	0
6	1	7	4
0	6	1	7

_____

_____

_____

_____

_____

Go Further ✎ What is the rule for adding 0 or 1 to a number? Give an example to explain your thinking.

_____

_____

_____

_____

_____

On today's activity: (Circle one) ✎ I did great! ✎ I did OK. ✎ I need help.

24 Name _____

Date

Get Started — Rule out two. Write why. Fill in the correct circle.

How many children have 1 pet?

(A) 1 child _____

(B) 3 children _____

(C) 5 children _____

(D) 7 children _____

PETS AT HOME

Number of Children

7
6
5
4
3
2
1
0

1 pet   2 pets   3 pets

Number of Pets

Today's Challenge

1. How many children have 3 pets?

(A) 1 child _____

(B) 2 children _____

(C) 3 children _____

(D) 4 children _____

2. How many children have 2 or more pets?

(A) 6 children _____

(B) 10 children _____

(C) 5 children _____

(D) 4 children _____

Total points for Today's Challenge: _____

On today's activity: (Circle one) — I did great! — I did OK. — I need help.

Name   Date   **25**

Today's Challenge

1. Use a yellow marker to color the even numbers on the chart below.

51	52	53	54	55	56	57	58	59	60
61	62	63	64	65	66	67	68	69	70
71	72	73	74	75	76	77	78	79	80
81	82	83	84	85	86	87	88	89	90
91	92	93	94	95	96	97	98	99	100

Skip count by twos to fill in the circles.
Write the word "even" or "odd."

2. 64 66 ◯ 70 ◯ 74   These numbers are _____.

3. 83 85 ◯ ◯ 91 ◯   These numbers are _____.

Go Further

5. Use a yellow marker or crayon to color the balloons with even numbers. Use another color to fill in the balloons with odd numbers.

On today's activity: (Circle one) I did great! I did OK. I need help.

Date

Today's Challenge — Draw a line to match the correct letter.

1. Find an addition problem with zero **and** an answer that equals 10.

   A. $10 + 0$

2. Find an addition with doubles that equals a sum of 10.

   B. $10 - 0$

3. Find a subtraction problem with zero **and** an answer that equals 10.

   C. $2 + 2 + 2 + 2 + 2$

4. Find a subtraction problem with 100 **and** an answer that equals 10.

   D. $5 + 5$

5. Find an addition problem with 2 plus a pair of doubles **and** an answer that equals 10.

   E. $2 + 4 + 4$

6. Find 5 addends with an answer that equals 10.

   F. $100 - 90$

Go Further

7. List 3 ways to show 9 using addition or subtraction problems.

   _____

   _____

   _____

On today's activity: (Circle one) — I did great! — I did OK. — I need help.

Name   **Date**   27

Today's Challenge — **For questions 1 and 2, circle** Yes **or** No.

1. :
   a. Two of me can fill a bathtub.   Yes   No

   b. You can use me to drink some milk.   Yes   No

   c. You can use me to hold paper clips.   Yes   No

   What is my name? _____

2. Clues:
   a. You can use me to fill the bathtub.   Yes   No

   b. You can use me to water the garden.   Yes   No

   c. You can use me to drink some milk.   Yes   No

   What is my name? _____

Go Further

3. Solve this riddle.

   Clues: · When I am full of water, I hold more than a cup.

   · When I am full of water, I hold more than the kitchen sink.

   · When I am full of water, I hold enough for you to take a bath.

   · What is my name? _____

4. Write your own riddle for a friend to solve.

   Clues: _____

   _____

   What is my name? _____

   Friend's name _____

On today's activity: (Circle one) — I did great!   I did OK.   I need help.

 **Name** _____

Date _____

Today's Challenge — Look for pairs of double addends. Write the addition sentences.

1	1	5	3
4	4	5	3
7	8	2	0
8	6	2	0

Double addends and their sums

_____ + _____ = _____

_____ + _____ = _____

_____ + _____ = _____

_____ + _____ = _____

Go Further — Create your own Math Jumble. Have a friend find and write five addition sentences with double addends.

_____

_____

_____

_____

Friend's name _____

On today's activity: (Circle one) — I did great! — I did OK. — I need help.

Name _____   **Date** _____   **29**

Get Started — Rule out two. Write why. Fill in the correct circle.

Bea is measuring the buttonhole on a jacket. Which unit best describes the length of the buttonhole?

(A) an inch _____   (B) a foot _____

(C) a yard _____   (D) a mile _____

Today's Challenge

1. Kim is building a fence around her garden. Which unit best describes the height of the fence?

   (A) inches _____ ☐

   (B) feet _____ ☐

   (C) tons _____ ☐

   (D) miles _____ ☐

2. The school nurse is measuring your height. Which unit best describes your height?

   (A) gallons _____ ☐

   (B) yards _____ ☐

   (C) inches _____ ☐

   (D) miles _____ ☐

Total points for Today's Challenge: _____

On today's activity: (Circle one) I did great! I did OK. I need help.

30 **Name**

Date

Today's Challenge 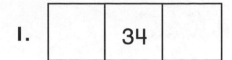 Fill in the missing numbers from the hundred chart. Look at the hundred chart in the back of your book if you need help.

1. | | 34 | |
   |---|---|---|

2. | | 56 | |
   |---|---|---|

3. | | 62 | |
   |---|---|---|

4. | | 48 | |
   |---|---|---|

5. | | 29 | |
   |---|---|---|

6. | | 83 | |
   |---|---|---|

Go Further  Fill in the missing numbers without using the hundred chart.

7. | | 83 | | | 86 | | |
   |---|---|---|---|---|---|---|

8. | | | | | 56 | | |
   |---|---|---|---|---|---|---|

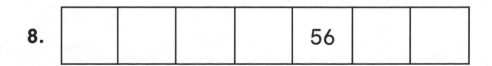

On today's activity: (Circle one) I did great! I did OK. I need help.

Name _____ **Date** _____

31

Today's Challenge ✏ Draw a line to match the correct letter.

1. 4 coins, worth a total of 25 cents

A. ⬤⬤⬤⬤⬤⬤

2. twin coins, worth a total of 20 cents

B. ⬤⬤

3. 6 coins, worth a total of 10 cents

C. ⬤⬤⬤⬤

4. 2 coins, where one is worth twice as much as the other

D. ⬤⬤⬤

5. 5 coins, worth a total of 50 cents

E. ⬤

6. 3 coins, worth a total of 15 cents

F. ⬤⬤⬤

7. 2 coins, worth a total of 50 cents

G. ⬤⬤

8. 3 coins, worth a total of 75 cents

H. ⬤⬤⬤⬤

Go Further ✏ Fill in the blanks to complete the riddle.
Give your riddle to a friend to solve.

9. I have _____ coins worth a total of _____ cents.
What coins do I have?

On today's activity: (Circle one) ✏ I did great! ✏ I did OK. ✏ I need help.

Today's Challenge

Fact Family for 2, 5, and 7

$$2 + 5 = 7 \qquad 5 + 2 = 7$$
$$7 - 2 = 5 \qquad 7 - 5 = 2$$

1. $6 + 4 = 10$	$\_\_ + \_\_ = 10$	**2.** $10 - 4 = 6$	$10 - \_\_ = \_\_$
3. $\_\_ + \_\_ = \_\_$	$7 + 1 = 8$	**4.** $8 - 7 = 1$	$8 - \_\_ = \_\_$
5. $2 + 7 = 10$	$\_\_ + \_\_ = \_\_$	**6.** $\_\_ - \_\_ = \_\_$	$9 - 2 = 7$
7. $\_\_ + \_\_ = \_\_$	$3 + 5 = 8$	**8.** $8 - 3 = 5$	$\_\_ - \_\_ = \_\_$

On today's activity: (Circle one) I did great! I did OK. I need help.

Name

Date

Today's Challenge

1. Loop a string of coins that totals 6¢.

2. Loop a string of coins that totals 7¢.

3. Loop a string of coins that totals 8¢.

4. Loop a string of coins that totals 9¢.

5. Loop a string of coins that totals 10¢.

Go Further

6. What is the total amount of money shown in the Math Jumble?
   Write how you found your answer.

_____

_____

_____

_____

_____

_____

On today's activity: (Circle one) I did great! I did OK. I need help.

Name

Date

Get Started — Rule out two. Write why. Fill in the correct circle.

Which item can slide?

A _____

B _____

C _____

D _____

Today's Challenge

1. Which item can slide?

A _____

B _____

C _____

D _____

2. Which item can slide and roll?

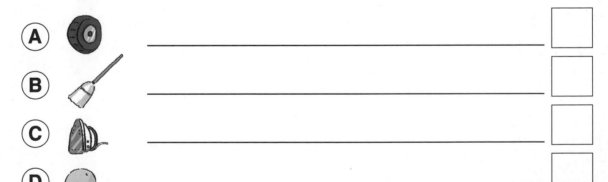

A _____

B _____

C _____

D _____

Total points for Today's Challenge: _____

On today's activity: (Circle one) ⬤ I did great! ⬤ I did OK. ⬤ I need help.

Name _____   **Date** _____

35

2, 4, 6, 8 Pattern Puzzler

Today's Challenge

1. Fill in the missing numbers from the hundred chart. Look at the hundred chart in the back of your book if you need help.

___	2	___	___	5	___	7	___	___	10
11	___	13	14	___	16	___	18	19	___

2.
___
12

3.
___
16

4.
___
15

5.
9
___

6.
8
___

Add.

7. 10 + 4 = _____   8. 10 + 1 = _____   9. 10 + 7 = _____

10. 2 + 10 = _____   11. 10 + 5 = _____   12. 8 + 10 = _____

Go Further   Fill in the blanks.

13. 4 + _____ = 14   14. _____ + 7 = 17   15. 1 + _____ = 11

On today's activity: (Circle one)   I did great!   I did OK.   I need help.

Name

Date

Today's Challenge   Draw a line to match the correct letter.

1. 43 and 10 more equals

2. 26 and 10 fewer equals

3. 90 and 20 fewer equals

4. 16 and 80 more equals

5. 64 and 10 fewer equals

6. 25 and 60 more equals

7. 73 and 50 fewer equals

8. 93 and 20 fewer equals

9. 96 and 40 fewer equals

10. 64 and 10 fewer equals

A. 70

B. 53

C. 16

D. 54

E. 85

F. 56

G. 73

H. 96

I. 23

J. 54

Go Further

11. Solve the puzzle. What is the final answer?

    Start: 43 → Add 10 → Add 10 → Add 10 → Subtract 1 →

    Subtract 1 → Subtract 10 _____

12. Now, write a puzzle of your own. Ask a friend to solve it.

    _____

    _____

On today's activity: (Circle one)   I did great!   I did OK.   I need help.

Name   **Date**   37

Today's Challenge — Use the pictures to answer questions 1 and 2.

1. **Clues:**

    a. Does it roll smoothly like a ball?   Yes   No

    b. Can it be stacked?   Yes   No

    c. Can it slide?   Yes   No

    d. Are all of the faces square?   Yes   No

What is my name? _____

2. **Clues:**

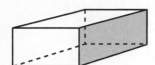

    a. Can it be stacked?   Yes   No

    b. Are all of the faces square?   Yes   No

    c. Can it slide?   Yes   No

    d. Does it roll smoothly like a ball?   Yes   No

What is my name? _____

Go Further

3. Solve this riddle.

Clues:

    · I have two round bases.

    · I can roll and I can slide.

    · What is my name? _____

4. Write your own riddle for a friend to solve.

Clues: _____

_____

What is my name? _____ Friend's name _____

On today's activity: (Circle one)   I did great!   I did OK.   I need help.

38 Name

Date

Today's Challenge Look for pairs of double addends with sums greater than 10. Write the addition sentences.

1	6	9	9
1	6	7	4
10	10	7	4
3	3	2	2

Double addends
(sums greater than 10)

_____ + _____ = _____

_____ + _____ = _____

_____ + _____ = _____

_____ + _____ = _____

Go Further Create your own Math Jumble. Have a friend find and write five addition sentences with double addends.

_____

_____

_____

_____

_____

Friend's name _____

On today's activity: (Circle one) I did great! I did OK. I need help.

Name **Date**

Get Started — Rule out two. Write why. Fill in the correct circle.

Hundreds Place	Tens Place	Ones Place
1	7	9
100 +	? +	9

What is the value of the digit 7 in 179?

A 7000 _____ **B** 700 _____

C 70 _____ **D** 7 _____

Today's Challenge

1. What is the value of the digit 8 in 842?

   A 8000 _____

   B 800 _____

   C 80 _____

   D 8 _____

2. What is the value of the digit 3 in 503?

   A 3000 _____

   B 300 _____

   C 30 _____

   D 3 _____

Total points for Today's Challenge: _____

On today's activity: (Circle one) — I did great! — I did OK. — I need help.

40 **Name** _____ **Date** _____

Today's Challenge 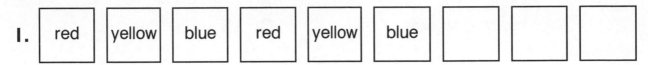 Use markers or crayons to color the blocks shown. Then complete each pattern by coloring in the rest of the blocks for each pattern.

1. | red | yellow | blue | red | yellow | blue | | | |

2. | orange | green | yellow | orange | green | yellow | | | |

3. | red | green | blue | red | green | blue | | | |

Go Further 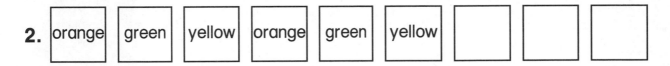 Use markers or crayons to color the blocks shown. Then fill in the blank blocks with the correct color(s).

4. | red | yellow | orange | red | yellow | | red | yellow | orange |

5. | blue | red | green | blue | | green | blue | | green |

6. | orange | | green | orange | blue | green | | blue | green |

On today's activity: (Circle one) I did great! I did OK. I need help.

Name　　　　　　　　**Date**

Today's Challenge — Draw a line to match the correct letter.

1. 0 plus 20 equals   **A.** 3

2. 11 take away 8 equals   **B.** 15

3. 12 minus 6 equals   **C.** 4

4. 11 minus 3 equals   **D.** 16

5. 9 take away 5 equals   **E.** 20

6. 6 plus 7 equals   **F.** 6

7. 7 plus 8 equals   **G.** 8

8. 12 take away 2 equals   **H.** 5

9. 9 take away 4 equals   **I.** 10

10. 8 plus 8 equals   **J.** 13

Go Further — Fill in the blanks.

11. 12 take away _____ equals 7.

12. 7 plus _____ equals 15.

13. _____ plus _____ equals 13.

On today's activity: (Circle one) — I did great! — I did OK. — I need help.

Date

Today's Challenge — **For each question, circle Yes or No.**

1. Clues:

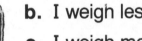

   a. I weigh less than a feather. Yes No

   b. I weigh less than a car. Yes No

   c. I weigh more than a sheet of paper. Yes No

   d. I weigh more than you. Yes No

   What is my name? _____

2. Clues:

   a. I weigh less than a feather. Yes No

   b. I weigh less than a car. Yes No

   c. I weigh more than a juice box. Yes No

   d. I weigh more than you. Yes No

   What is my name? _____

Go Further

3. Solve this riddle.

   Clues:

   · I am heavier than a sheet of paper.

   · I am lighter than a ton of bricks.

   · I cannot be blown away.

   · I cannot give you a lift.

   · What is my name? _____

4. Write your own riddle for a friend to solve.

   Clues: _____

   _____

   What is my name? _____ Friend's name _____

On today's activity: (Circle one) — I did great! — I did OK. — I need help.

Name _____ **Date** _____ 43

Today's Challenge Look for numbers that can be added using the doubles plus 1 strategy. Write the addition sentences in the table.

4	3	8	7
5	4	5	6
6	7	4	1
9	8	3	2

Doubles plus 1	
$3 + 4 = 3 + 3 + 1 = 7$	

Go Further Create your own Math Jumble. Have a friend find and write five addition sentences using the doubles plus 1 strategy.

Friend's name ______________________

On today's activity: (Circle one) I did great! I did OK. I need help.

Name

Date

Get Started — **Rule out two. Write why. Fill in the correct circle.**

Which unit best describes the weight of a car?

(A) ounce _____ (B) pound _____

(C) ton _____ (D) mile _____

Today's Challenge

1. Which unit best describes the weight of a feather?

   (A) inch _____ ☐

   (B) ounce _____ ☐

   (C) pound _____ ☐

   (D) ton _____ ☐

2. Which unit best describes the weight of a bag of flour?

   (A) quart _____ ☐

   (B) ounce _____ ☐

   (C) pound _____ ☐

   (D) ton _____ ☐

Total points for Today's Challenge: _____

On today's activity: (Circle one) — I did great! — I did OK. — I need help.

Name   Date   45

Today's Challenge

1. Look at the numbers below. Circle the number pairs with a difference of 2.

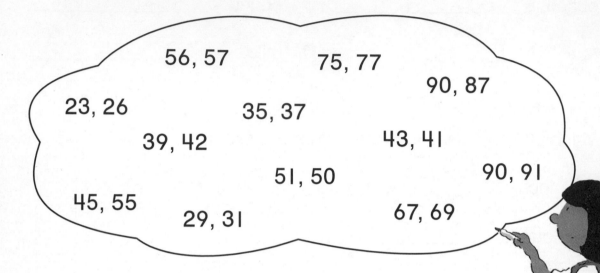

56, 57   75, 77

90, 87

23, 26   35, 37

39, 42   43, 41

51, 50   90, 91

45, 55   67, 69

29, 31

For each problem, write a number so that the pair of numbers has a difference of 2.

2. 53, _____   **3.** 67, _____   **4.** 89, _____

5. 49, _____   **6.** 71, _____   **7.** 95, _____

Go Further

8. Write three pairs of consecutive odd numbers that have a difference of 2. Use numbers between 50 and 100.

_____, _____   _____, _____   _____, _____

On today's activity: (Circle one) I did great! I did OK. I need help.

46   **Name**

Date

Math Maze

Today's Challenge

Write the time next to each clock. Choose answers from the box.

45 minutes past 4 o'clock	10 o'clock	12:45
half past 4	3 o'clock	7:15
12 noon	6 o'clock	11:15

1.  _____

2. _____

3.  _____

4. _____

5.  _____

6. _____

7.  _____

8. _____

Go Further

9. Draw the time you get up in the morning.

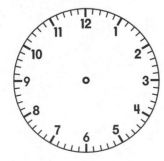

10. Draw the time you go to sleep at night.

On today's activity: (Circle one) — I did great! — I did OK. — I need help.

Name _____ Date _____

Today's Challenge

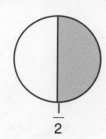 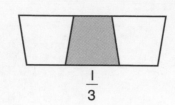 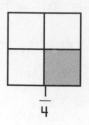

$\frac{1}{2}$ $\frac{1}{3}$ $\frac{1}{4}$

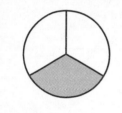

1. _____

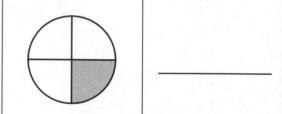

2. _____

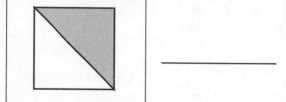

3. _____

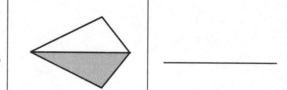

4. _____

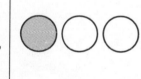

5. _____

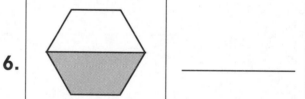

6. _____

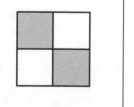

7. _____

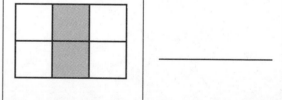

8. _____

On today's activity: (Circle one) I did great! I did OK. I need help.

Today's Challenge Look for three addends with sums less than 18. Write the facts below.

2	4	6	6
5	3	7	2
1	3	4	5
6	4	2	1

Sums less than 18

_____ + _____ + _____ = _____

_____ + _____ + _____ = _____

_____ + _____ + _____ = _____

_____ + _____ + _____ = _____

Go Further Create your own Math Jumble for three addends. Have a friend write five addition sentences with three addends whose sum is less than 18.

_____

_____

_____

_____

Friend's name _____

On today's activity: (Circle one) I did great! I did OK. I need help.

Name **Date**

Get Started — Rule out two. Write why. Fill in the correct circle.

Which item will roll?

Ⓐ _____ Ⓑ _____

Ⓒ _____ Ⓓ _____

Today's Challenge

1. Which item will roll?

Ⓐ _____ ☐

Ⓑ _____ ☐

Ⓒ _____ ☐

Ⓓ _____ ☐

2. Which solid will roll?

Ⓐ _____ ☐

Ⓑ _____ ☐

Ⓒ _____ ☐

Ⓓ _____ ☐

Total points for Today's Challenge: _____

On today's activity: (Circle one) — I did great! — I did OK. — I need help.

2, 4, 6, 8 Pattern Puzzler

Today's Challenge Write < , > , or = to make each number sentence true.

1. 10 + 3 ◯ 10

10 + 3 ◯ 11

10 + 3 ◯ 12

10 + 3 ◯ 13

10 + 3 ◯ 14

2. 9 + 5 ◯ 17

9 + 6 ◯ 17

9 + 7 ◯ 17

9 + 8 ◯ 17

9 + 9 ◯ 17

3. 8 + 4 ◯ 16

8 + 5 ◯ 16

8 + 6 ◯ 16

8 + 7 ◯ 16

8 + 8 ◯ 16

4. 9 + 4 ◯ 10

9 + 4 ◯ 11

9 + 4 ◯ 12

9 + 4 ◯ 13

9 + 4 ◯ 14

5. 7 + 10 ◯ 16

7 + 9 ◯ 16

7 + 8 ◯ 16

7 + 7 ◯ 16

7 + 6 ◯ 16

6. 9 + 4 ◯ 10 + 3

9 + 5 ◯ 10 + 4

9 + 6 ◯ 10 + 5

9 + 7 ◯ 10 + 6

9 + 8 ◯ 10 + 7

Go Further

7. _____ + _____ > 24

8. _____ + _____ < 24

On today's activity: (Circle one) I did great! I did OK. I need help.

Name _____ Date _____

Today's Challenge — Draw a line to match the correct letter.

1. a solid that is round all over

A.

2. the name of this shape

B.

3. a solid that is round on one end and pointed on the other

C.

4. flat shape that is round

D.

5. the name of this shape

E. rectangle

6. a solid that has 4 rectangles and 2 squares

F.

7. the shape of a cylinder

G. triangle

Go Further

8. Draw 2 solids and 2 flat shapes. Label the figures.

On today's activity: (Circle one) — I did great! — I did OK. — I need help.

Date

Today's Challenge

Figure	Area	Figure	Area	Figure	Area
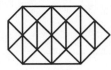	6 squares		23 triangles		9 rectangles

1.		_____ squares	2.	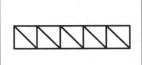	_____ triangles
3.		_____ rectangles	4.		_____ trapezoids
5.		_____ triangles	6.	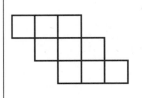	_____ squares
7.	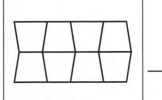	_____ trapezoids	8.		_____ rectangles

On today's activity: (Circle one) 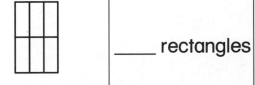 I did great! ▬ I did OK. ▬ I need help.

Name   **Date**

Today's Challenge
Look for pairs of numbers with sums greater than 10. Write the addition sentences.

8	3	5	9
5	7	4	7
4	6	8	6
9	3	5	9

_____

_____

_____

_____

_____

Go Further
Create your own Math Jumble. Have a friend find five facts with sums greater than 10.

_____

_____

_____

_____

Friend's name _____

On today's activity: (Circle one) I did great! I did OK. I need help.

Name

Date

Get Started — Rule out two. Write why. Fill in the correct circle.

Gordan counted 66 red cars on the way to the beach. He counted 22 more red cars on the way home. How many red cars did Gordan count?

(A) $66 - 22 = 44$ _____ (B) $88 - 22 = 66$ _____

(C) $88 - 44 = 22$ _____ (D) $66 + 22 = 88$ _____

Today's Challenge

1. Marva has 38 baseball cards. Travis has 41. How many cards do they have altogether?

(A) $38 + 41 = 79$ _____ ☐

(B) $30 + 40 = 70$ _____ ☐

(C) $8 + 1 = 9$ _____ ☐

(D) $41 - 38 = 3$ _____ ☐

2. Madison has 25 paper cups. Taylor has 20. How many cups do they have together?

(A) $25 - 20 = 5$ _____ ☐

(B) $20 + 20 = 40$ _____ ☐

(C) $25 + 20 = 45$ _____ ☐

(D) $25 + 25 = 50$ _____ ☐

Total points for Today's Challenge: _____

On today's activity: (Circle one) I did great! I did OK. I need help.

Name _____ Date _____

2, 4, 6, 8 Pattern Puzzler

Today's Challenge

November						
Sun	Mon	Tue	Wed	Thu	Fri	Sat
	1	2	3	4	5	6
7	8	9	10	11	12	13
14	15	16	17	18	19	20
21	22	23	24	25	26	27
28	29	30				

1. Use orange, green, and yellow markers or crayons to color the calendar. Use the pattern orange, green, yellow to color the numbers 1, 2, and 3. Then repeat the pattern for the numbers 4, 5, and 6. Continue until the whole calendar is complete.

2. Look at all the yellow numbers.
   Write them on the blanks.
   What pattern do you see?

   _____, _____, _____, _____, _____, _____, _____, _____, _____, _____

   _____

Go Further

3. Look at the orange numbers on the calendar. Write them on the blanks. What pattern do you see?

   _____, _____, _____, _____, _____, _____, _____, _____, _____, _____, _____

   _____

On today's activity: (Circle one) I did great! I did OK. I need help.

Date

Math Maze

Today's Challenge — Draw a line to match the correct letter.

1. What is half of 12 inches?
2. What is half the number of legs on a cat?
3. What is half of 60 minutes?
4. What is half of 52 weeks?
5. What is half the number of years in a century?
6. What is half of the distance of 100 yards?
7. What is half the number of wheels on an 18-wheeler truck?
8. What is half of 10 pennies?
9. What Is half the number of pages in a 48-page book?
10. What is half of 90 seconds?

A. 2 legs
B. 26 weeks
C. 50 yards
D. 6 inches
E. 30 minutes
F. 45 seconds
G. 50 years
H. 9 wheels
I. 5 pennies
J. 24 pages

Go Further — Loop the items to show half.

11.

12.

13.

14.

On today's activity: (Circle one) — I did great! — I did OK. — I need help.

Name

Date

Go Further — Follow the directions to cross out the times.

- Cross out all times that show an even number hour with ":00" minutes.

- Cross out all times that show 15 minutes after an odd number hour.

- Cross out all times that show 15 minutes after an even number hour.

1. What time is left? _____

2. What are two other names for 12:00?

_____ and _____

On today's activity: (Circle one) — I did great! — I did OK. — I need help.

Today's Challenge

1. Loop a string of coins that equals 11¢.

2. Loop a string of coins that equals 22¢.

3. Loop a string of coins that equals 23¢.

4. Loop a string of coins that equals 15¢.

5. Loop a string of coins that equals 17¢.

Go Further

6. What is the total amount of money shown in the Math Jumble?
   Write how you found your answer.

_____

_____

_____

_____

_____

_____

On today's activity: (Circle one) I did great! I did OK. I need help.

Name   **Date**

Get Started — Rule out two. Write why. Fill in the correct circle.

Mr. Gomez cut 29 roses from his garden. What is another way to write 29?

A 20 + 19 _____ **B** 2 + 9 _____

C 10 + 9 _____ **D** 20 + 9 _____

Today's Challenge

1. Darlene has 48 cupcakes for the bake sale. What is another way to write 48?

    A 40 + 8 _____ ☐

    B 4 + 8 _____ ☐

    C 4 + 80 _____ ☐

    D 20 + 18 _____ ☐

2. Damien put 75 pennies in his piggy bank. What is another way to write 75?

    A 70 + 5 _____ ☐

    B 70 + 15 _____ ☐

    C 7 + 5 _____ ☐

    D 75 + 5 _____ ☐

Total points for Today's Challenge: _____

On today's activity: (Circle one) — I did great! — I did OK. — I need help.

60 **Name** _____ **Date** _____

Today's Challenge

1. Look at the completed addition problems on this page. Without adding, circle the incorrect sums.

> **Name:** Jason
>
> | 1. 8
+ 6
14 | 2. 14
+ 8
23 | 3. 28
+ 16
44 | 4. 32
+ 16
49 | 5. 40
+ 32
72 |
> |---|---|---|---|---|
> | 6. 52
+ 14
67 | 7. 60
+ 34
94 | 8. 72
+ 14
87 | 9. 66
+ 22
88 | 10. 54
+ 38
93 |

Look at Jason's homework. Correct the addition problems that have the wrong sum.

2.   **3.**   **4.**   **5.**   **6.**

+ _____   + _____   + _____   + _____   + _____

Go Further

7. Look at the three addition problems below. Circle the one with the correct sum.

236 + 2 237	20 + 14 34	112 + 6 97

On today's activity: (Circle one) I did great! I did OK. I need help.

Name _____   **Date** _____   61

Today's Challenge — Choose answers from the box to fill in the blanks.

4 pennies	20 minutes	45 minutes
14 pounds	55 degrees	$15	4 tons

1. At noon, the outside temperature is 60 degrees. Later, it drops 5 degrees. What is the new temperature? _____

2. Each song on the CD is 2 minutes long. How long will it take to play all 10 songs? _____

3. Leslie has 32 pennies. She puts them in 8 equal groups. How many pennies are in each group? _____

4. Ed's new car weighs 2 tons. Justine's new car weighs the same. How much do the two cars weigh together? _____

5. Ben earns $1 a day dog walking. He works for 15 days. How much money will he have? _____

6. As a puppy, Maggie weighed 3 pounds. Now, she weighs 17 pounds. How much weight did she gain? _____

7. Ella goes to swim class at 3 o'clock. The class ends at 3: 45. How long is the lesson? _____

Go Further

8. Write a simple word problem. Give it to a friend to solve.

_____

_____

On today's activity: (Circle one) — I did great! — I did OK. — I need help.

Date

Today's Challenge — For questions 1 and 2, circle **Yes** or **No**.

1. Clues:

   a. Does it roll? Yes No

   b. Can it be stacked? Yes No

   c. Can it slide? Yes No

   d. Does it have 1 base? Yes No

What is my name? _____

2. Clues:

   a. Can it be stacked? Yes No

   b. Does it have 2 bases? Yes No

   c. Can it slide? Yes No

   d. Does it roll? Yes No

What is my name? _____

Go Further

3. Solve this riddle.

Clues:

   · I am a solid.

   · Use my base to trace a circle.

   · I can hold 2 of your favorite scoops.

   · What is my name? _____

4. Write your own riddle for a friend to solve.

Clues: _____

_____

What is my name? _____ Friend's name _____

On today's activity: (Circle one) I did great! I did OK. I need help.

Name   Date   **63**

Today's Challenge Look for strings of numbers to make subtraction facts. Write the facts you find.

Subtraction facts

_____

_____

_____

_____

_____

_____

_____

8	3	9	3
1	5	2	6
7	4	3	2
6	1	5	4

Go Further Now look for strings of numbers to make addition facts.

_____   _____

_____   _____

_____   _____

_____   _____

On today's activity: (Circle one) I did great! I did OK. I need help.

Date

Get Started ✏ Rule out two. Write why. Fill in the correct circle.

Alberto got 90 points on his spelling test this week. Last week he got 70 points. How many more points did he score this week?

(A) 10 points _____   **(B)** 20 points _____

(C) 30 points _____   **(D)** 90 points _____

Today's Challenge

1. Cameron did 20 sit-ups in gym class today. Peter did 50 sit-ups. How many more sit-ups did Peter do?

   (A) 7 sit-ups _____ ☐

   (B) 30 sit-ups _____ ☐

   (C) 5 sit-ups _____ ☐

   (D) 70 sit-ups _____ ☐

2. Maureen played a math game for 10 minutes. Gwen played for 60 minutes. How many more minutes did Gwen play?

   (A) 20 minutes _____ ☐

   (B) 30 minutes _____ ☐

   (C) 50 minutes _____ ☐

   (D) 100 minutes _____ ☐

Total points for Today's Challenge: _____

On today's activity: (Circle one) ✏ I did great! ✏ I did OK. ✏ I need help.

Name _____   **Date** _____   **65**

2, 4, 6, 8 Pattern Puzzler

Today's Challenge — Complete each pattern. Draw the correct shapes.

1. ◯ ▢ ▢ △ ◯ ◯ ▢ △ ◯ ▢ △ _____ _____ _____

2. △ ▯ ▢ ◯ △ ▮ ▢ ◯ △ ▯ ◯ _____ _____ _____

3. ▢ ▯ ◯ ▬ ▢ ▮ ◯ ▬ ▢ ▯ ◯ ▬ _____ _____ _____

Go Further

4. Draw a pattern of your own using three different shapes.

_____ _____ _____ _____ _____ _____

_____ _____ _____ _____ _____ _____

5. Describe your pattern.

_____

On today's activity: (Circle one) — I did great! — I did OK. — I need help.

Date

Today's Challenge — Use mental math to add.
Draw a line to match the correct letter.

1. 14 + 10   A. 41

2. 85 + 10   B. 95

3. 29 + 10   C. 41

4. 10 + 44   D. 54

5. 31 + 10   E. 69

6. 62 + 10   F. 39

7. 10 + 28   G. 80

8. 31 + 10   H. 24

9. 70 + 10   I. 38

10. 59 + 10   J. 72

Go Further

11. _____ + 10 = 37   12. 10 + _____ = 48

On today's activity: (Circle one) ⬤ I did great! ⬤ I did OK. ⬤ I need help.

Name   Date

Today's Challenge

Figure	Perimeter

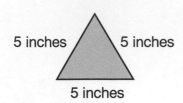

5 inches + 5 inches + 5 inches = 15 inches

1.	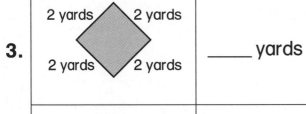	____ inches	**2.**	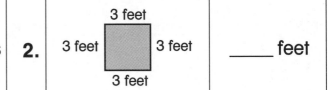	____ feet
3.	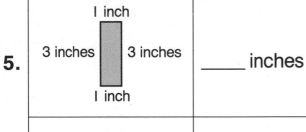	____ yards	**4.**	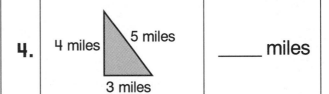	____ miles
5.	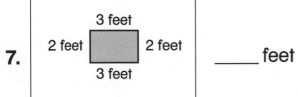	____ inches	**6.**	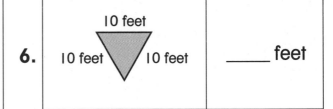	____ feet
7.	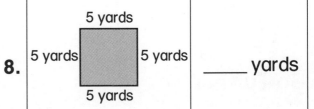	____ feet	**8.**		____ yards

On today's activity: (Circle one) I did great! I did OK. I need help.

Date _____

Today's Challenge
Look for three numbers you can use to subtract twice in a row. Write the subtraction sentences below.

Remember: the difference at the end must be 0 or greater!

20	11	5	3
6	5	4	2
10	17	8	1
13	3	9	0

Subtraction sentences

_____ – _____ – _____ = _____

_____ – _____ – _____ = _____

_____ – _____ – _____ = _____

_____ – _____ – _____ = _____

_____ – _____ – _____ = _____

Go Further
Create your own Math Jumble. Include sets of three numbers you can subtract twice in a row. Have a friend write subtraction sentences for the numbers.

_____

_____

_____

_____

_____

Friend's name _____

On today's activity: (Circle one) I did great! I did OK. I need help.

Name

Date

69

Rule Out Two

Rule Out Two

Week 14 • Activity 70

Get Started — Rule out two. Write why. Fill in the correct circle.

How many inches are equal to 2 feet?

(A) 48 inches _____

(B) 36 inches _____

(C) 24 inches _____

(D) 12 inches _____

Item	Length in inches	Length in feet
	12 inches	1 foot
	24 inches	2 feet
	36 inches	3 feet
	48 inches	4 feet

Today's Challenge

1. How many feet are equal to 36 inches?

   (A) 1 foot _____ ☐

   (B) 4 feet _____ ☐

   (C) 2 feet _____ ☐

   (D) 3 feet _____ ☐

2. The jump rope is 36 inches long. Which item is longer?

   (A) _____ ☐

   (B) _____ ☐

   (C) _____ ☐

   (D) _____ ☐

Total points for Today's Challenge: _____

On today's activity: (Circle one) — I did great! — I did OK. — I need help.

70 Name _____   Date _____

Today's Challenge

1. Look at each pair of numbers on the path. Color the stones that show a difference of 3.

For each problem, write a number so that the pair of numbers has a difference of 3.

2. 18, _____   **3.** 45, _____   **4.** 27, _____

5. 57, _____   **6.** 39, _____   **7.** 51, _____

Go Further

8. Does the pair 33 and 63 have a difference of 3? Explain your answer.

_____

_____

On today's activity: (Circle one) I did great!   I did OK.   I need help.

Name _____   **Date** _____   71

Today's Challenge — Draw a line to match the correct letter.

1. 15 plus ☐ equals 19?

2. 25 plus ☐ equals 27?

3. 20 plus ☐ equals 21?

4. 10 plus ☐ equals 12?

5. 22 plus ☐ equals 29?

6. 14 plus ☐ equals 23?

7. 10 plus ☐ equals 15?

8. 20 plus ☐ equals 31?

9. 29 plus ☐ equals 29?

10. 14 plus ☐ equals 28?

A. 2

B. 7

C. 9

D. 4

E. 5

F. 11

G. 14

H. 1

I. 0

J. 2

Go Further

11. 27 + _____ = 31   **12.** 15 + _____ = 22   **13.** 48 + _____ = 51

On today's activity: (Circle one) I did great! I did OK. I need help.

Date

Today's Challenge

Addition	Sum		Addition	Sum
$3 + 3 + 3 \rightarrow$	9		$2 + 2 + 2 + 2 \rightarrow$	8

	Addition	Sum		Addition	Sum
1.	$5 + 5 + 5 + 5$	_____	**2.**	$4+4+4+4+4+4$	_____
3.	$2 + 2 + 2 =$	_____	**4.**	$6 + 6 + 6 =$	_____
5.	$7 + 7 + 7$	_____	**6.**	$8 + 8 + 8 + 8$	_____
7.	_____	14	**8.**	_____	25

On today's activity: (Circle one) 🎗 I did great! 🎗 I did OK. 🎗 I need help.

Name   **Date**   73

Today's Challenge Look for strings of numbers. First, find two numbers whose sum is 10. Then, string on a third number. Write the addition sentences.

4	7	1	6
6	5	5	8
2	9	3	2
9	1	7	4

Addition sentences

6 + 4 + 7 = 17

___ + ___ + ___ = ___

___ + ___ + ___ = ___

___ + ___ + ___ = ___

___ + ___ + ___ = ___

___ + ___ + ___ = ___

Go Further Create your own Math Jumble. Use the one above as a guide. Have a friend write five addition sentences with three addends.

_____

_____

_____

_____

_____

Friend's name _____

On today's activity: (Circle one) I did great! I did OK. I need help.

74 Name

Date

Get Started — Rule out two. Write why. Fill in the correct circle.

Which of the 4 shapes are exactly the same?

(A) A and D _____

(B) B and C _____

(C) B and D _____

(D) A and B _____

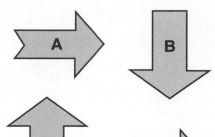

Today's Challenge

1. Which of the 4 shapes are exactly the same?

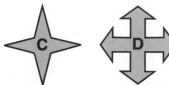

(A) A and C _____

(B) A and B _____

(C) B and C _____

(D) B and D _____

2. Which one of the 4 shapes is not exactly the same as the others?

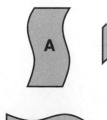

(A) A _____

(B) B _____

(C) C _____

(D) D _____

Total points for Today's Challenge: _____

On today's activity: (Circle one) I did great! I did OK. I need help.

Name _____   Date _____

2, 4, 6, 8 Pattern Puzzler

Today's Challenge

1. Look at each pair of numbers on the fish. Use a yellow marker or crayon to color each fish that has a pair of numbers with a difference of 2.

2. How many fish with a difference of 2 did the bear catch? _____

3. Use another color marker or crayon to color the fish that have pairs of numbers with a difference greater than 2.

4. How many fish with a difference greater than 2 did the bear catch? _____

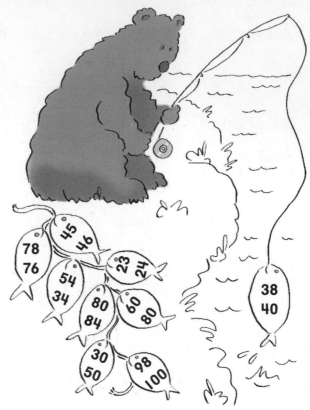

Go Further

5. Find neighboring numbers that have a difference of 2. Circle those numbers to move from START to END.

START ⓐ(76)→(78) 58 68 48 78 94 99

73 (80) 82 84 88 74 98 100 **END**

53 84 72 86 92 94 96 97

33 87 76 88 90 91 93 95

On today's activity: (Circle one) I did great! I did OK. I need help.

76 **Name**

Date

Today's Challenge — Draw a line to match the correct letter.

1. 5 cents

2. 4 cents

3. 20 cents

4. 36 cents

5. 25 cents

6. 9 cents

7. 15 cents

8. 2 cents

9. 75 cents

10. 50 cents

A.

B.

C.

D.

E.

F.

G.

H.

I.

J.

Go Further

11. List the money below in order, from the least value to the greatest value.

_____

On today's activity: (Circle one) I did great! I did OK. I need help.

Name   **Date**

Today's Challenge

	Shape	Name		Shape	Name
1.	▭	_____	2.	◣	_____
3.	●	_____	4.	⏢	_____
5.	(draw figure)	Rhombus	6.	(draw figure)	Square
7.	(draw figure)	Oval	8.	(draw figure)	Circle

On today's activity: (Circle one) ❯ I did great! ❯ I did OK. ❯ I need help.

Date

Today's Challenge — Fill in the grid with the numbers from the Math Jumble Activity poster.

Sums of 12 with 2 addends	Sums of 12 with more than 2 addends

Go Further — Create your own Math Jumble. Have a friend write five facts with sums of 12.

_____

_____

_____

_____

_____

Friend's name _____

On today's activity: (Circle one) — I did great! — I did OK. — I need help.

Name _____   Date _____

Get Started — Rule out two. Write why. Fill in the correct circle.

There are 4 puppies in the kennel. Three of them have spots. Which fraction describes the puppies with spots?

(A) $\frac{1}{3}$ _____

(B) $\frac{3}{3}$ _____

(C) $\frac{3}{4}$ _____

(D) $\frac{1}{4}$ _____

Today's Challenge

1. One puppy came out of the kennel. Which fraction describes the puppy not in the kennel?

(A) $\frac{1}{3}$ _____ ☐

(B) $\frac{1}{4}$ _____ ☐

(C) $\frac{3}{3}$ _____ ☐

(D) $\frac{3}{4}$ _____ ☐

2. Three puppies have collars. Which fraction describes the puppies with collars?

(A) $\frac{1}{3}$ _____ ☐

(B) $\frac{1}{4}$ _____ ☐

(C) $\frac{3}{3}$ _____ ☐

(D) $\frac{3}{4}$ _____ ☐

Total points for Today's Challenge: _____

On today's activity: (Circle one) — I did great! — I did OK. — I need help.

80 Name

Date

Today's Challenge — Skip count by tens to complete each list.

1. 300	2. 600	3. 800	4. 500
310	_____	810	_____
320	620	_____	_____
330	_____	_____	_____
_____	640	_____	_____
_____	_____	_____	_____
360	_____	_____	_____
_____	_____	_____	_____
_____	680	_____	_____
390	_____	_____	_____

Go Further

6. Skip count by tens. Connect the dots in the picture between 350 and 450.

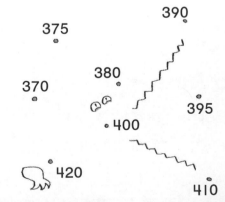

305

375

362

360

390

380

370

395

START
350

400

450
END

440   430   420   410

445

On today's activity: (Circle one) — I did great! — I did OK. — I need help.

Name   **Date**

Math Maze

Today's Challenge — Draw a line to match the correct letter.

1. What time is 30 minutes after 12:30?

A.

2. What time is 30 minutes after 6:30?

B.

3. What time is half an hour after noon?

C.

4. What time is half an hour after 8:00?

D.

5. What time is 30 minutes after 4:00?

E.

6. What time is 30 minutes after 11:15?

F.

7. What time is 30 minutes after 8:30?

G.

8. What time is half an hour after 9:15?

H.

Go Further

9. The time is 8:30.
In 1 hour it will be _____:_____.

10. The time is noon.
In 30 minutes it will be _____:_____.

On today's activity: (Circle one) I did great! I did OK. I need help.

Date

Today's Challenge — **For questions 1 and 2, circle Yes or No.**

1. **Clues:**

   a. I am used for baking and cooking.   Yes   No

   b. I am small enough to carry in one hand.   Yes   No

   c. I am equal to a half pint.   Yes   No

   What is my name? _____

2. **Clues:**

   a. I can be poured into many little cups.   Yes   No

   b. I am very heavy when filled to the top.   Yes   No

   c. I am more than 1 cup.   Yes   No

   What is my name? _____

Go Further

3. Solve this riddle.

   Clues:

   · It takes 4 cups to fill me up.

   · I am more than a pint.

   · My name rhymes with "wart."

   · What is my name? _____

4. Write your own riddle for a friend to solve.

   Clues: _____

   _____

   What is my name? _____

   Friend's name _____

On today's activity: (Circle one) — I did great! I did OK. I need help.

Name _____   **Date** _____

Today's Challenge — Fill in the grid with the numbers from the Math Jumble Activity poster.

Sums of 13 with 2 addends	Sums of 13 with more than 2 addends

Go Further — Create your own Math Jumble. Have a friend find five facts with sums of 13.

_____

_____

_____

_____

_____

Friend's name _____

On today's activity: (Circle one) — I did great! — I did OK. — I need help.

Get Started — Rule out two. Write why.
Fill in the correct circle.

The distance from the floor to the doorknob is
36 inches. How many feet are equal to 36 inches?

Inches		Feet
12 inches	=	1 foot
24 inches	=	2 feet
36 inches	=	3 feet
48 inches	=	4 feet
60 inches	=	5 feet

(A) 2 feet _____   **(B)** 3 feet _____

(C) 4 feet _____   **(D)** 5 feet _____

Today's Challenge

1. Manuel is now 60 inches tall. How many feet are equal to 60 inches?

(A) 2 feet _____ ☐

(B) 3 feet _____ ☐

(C) 4 feet _____ ☐

(D) 5 feet _____ ☐

2. The chain is 48 inches long. How many feet are equal to 48 inches?

(A) 2 feet _____ ☐

(B) 3 feet _____ ☐

(C) 4 feet _____ ☐

(D) 5 feet _____ ☐

Total points for Today's Challenge: _____

On today's activity: (Circle one) ✐ I did great! ✐ I did OK. ✐ I need help.

Name _____   Date _____   85

Today's Challenge

1. Skip count by fives. Use a yellow marker or crayon to circle all those numbers. Start with the number 5.

1	2	3	4	5	6	7	8	9	10
11	12	13	14	15	16	17	18	19	20
21	22	23	24	25	26	27	28	29	30
31	32	33	34	35	36	37	38	39	40
41	42	43	44	45	46	47	48	49	50
51	52	53	54	55	56	57	58	59	60
61	62	63	64	65	66	67	68	69	70
71	72	73	74	75	76	77	78	79	80
81	82	83	84	85	86	87	88	89	90
91	92	93	94	95	96	97	98	99	100

2. Look again at the hundred chart. What pattern do you see? Name the digits that are always in the ones place.

Go Further

3. Skip count by fives from 5 to 100. Circle those numbers as you say them. Find the path from START to END.

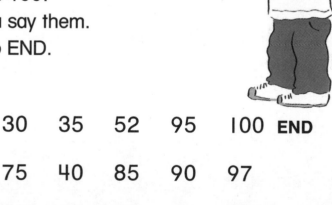

START	⑤	53	25	30	35	52	95	100 **END**
	⑩→⑮	20	75	40	85	90	97	
	18	35	63	50	45	80	75	85
	57	45	75	55	60	65	70	82

On today's activity: (Circle one) I did great! I did OK. I need help.

Today's Challenge — Draw a line to match the correct letter.

1. 20 more than 30 equals   **A.** 95

2. 2 more than 46 equals   **B.** 27

3. 10 more than 85 equals   **C.** 44

4. 2 more than 25 equals   **D.** 97

5. 10 greater than 34 equals   **E.** 74

6. 3 less than 100 equals   **F.** 50

7. 4 more than 70 equals   **G.** 34

8. 5 less than 39 equals   **H.** 48

9. 1 less than 21 equals   **I.** 20

10. 10 less than 70 equals   **J.** 60

Go Further — Which number is greater? Circle the greater number in each pair.

11. 1 less than 50 or
    1 greater than 60

12. 10 greater than 70 or
    1 less than 80

13. 4 greater than 30 or
    1 greater than 30

14. 4 greater than 30 or
    1 less than 30

On today's activity: (Circle one) — I did great! — I did OK. — I need help.

Name _____

Date _____

Today's Challenge — For questions 1 and 2, circle Yes or No.

1. Clues:

a. Does it roll smoothly like a ball?   Yes   No

b. Can it be stacked?   Yes   No

c. Does it have any triangular faces?   Yes   No

d. Are all of the faces square?   Yes   No

What is my name? _____

2. Clues:

a. Can it be stacked?   Yes   No

b. Are all of the faces rectangles?   Yes   No

c. Can it slide?   Yes   No

d. Does it roll smoothly like a ball?   Yes   No

What is my name? _____

Go Further

3. Solve this riddle.

Clues:

· I have six edges.

· My faces come to a point.

· If you trace one of my faces you will get a triangle.

· What is my name? _____

4. Write your own riddle for a friend to solve.

Clues: _____

_____

What is my name? _____   Friend's name _____

On today's activity: (Circle one) — I did great! — I did OK. — I need help.

Today's Challenge — **Fill in the grid with the numbers from the Math Jumble Activity poster.**

Sums of 14 with 2 addends	Sums of 14 with more than 2 addends

Go Further — **Create your own Math Jumble. Have a friend find and write five facts with sums of 14.**

_____

_____

_____

_____

_____

Friend's name _____

On today's activity: (Circle one) — I did great! — I did OK. — I need help.

Name   **Date**

Get Started — Rule out two. Write why. Fill in the correct circle.

There are 236 tiles on the bathroom floor. What is another way to write 236?

(A) 2 + 3 + 6 _____   (B) 200 + 30 + 6 _____

(C) 20 + 30 + 6 _____   (D) 200 + 300 + 60 _____

Today's Challenge

1. Luke lives in Apartment 379. What is another way to write 379?

(A) 300 + 70 + 9 _____ ☐

(B) 30 + 70 + 9 _____ ☐

(C) 300 + 700 + 900 _____ ☐

(D) 300 + 7 + 9 _____ ☐

2. Marisa flew 642 miles to visit California. What is another way to write 642?

(A) 60 + 40 + 2 _____ ☐

(B) 600 + 400 + 200 _____ ☐

(C) 600 + 40 + 2 _____ ☐

(D) 600 + 40 + 20 _____ ☐

Total points for Today's Challenge: _____

On today's activity: (Circle one) — I did great! — I did OK. — I need help.

90 **Name**

Date

2, 4, 6, 8 Pattern Puzzler

Today's Challenge

1. Use the pattern orange, blue, blue, yellow to color the numbers 1, 2, 3, and 4. Then, repeat the pattern of colors for the numbers, 5, 6, 7, and 8. Continue until the whole calendar is complete.

March						
Sun	Mon	Tue	Wed	Thu	Fri	Sat
				1	2	3
4	5	6	7	8	9	10
11	12	13	14	15	16	17
18	19	20	21	22	23	24
25	26	27	28	29	30	31

2. Look at all the yellow numbers. Write them on the blanks. What number pattern do you see?

4, _____, _____, _____, _____, _____, _____

_____

_____

_____

Go Further

3. Find March 4 on the calendar. Look at the diagonal downward. Use the yellow numbers on this diagonal to fill in the blanks.

4, _____, 20, _____

What number pattern do you see?

_____

On today's activity: (Circle one) I did great! I did OK. I need help.

Name _____ Date _____

Today's Challenge — Choose answers from the box to fill in the blanks.

26	10	2	31
1000	50	29	20

1. The number of fingers and toes on each person is _____.

2. The number of socks in a pair is _____.

3. The number of states in the United States is _____.

4. The number of days in February in a leap year is _____.

5. The number of years in a millennium is _____.

6. The number of letters in the English alphabet is _____.

7. The date in December for New Year's Eve is _____.

8. The number of years in a decade is _____.

Go Further — Fill in the blanks.

9. The number of letters in my name is _____.

10. I am _____ years old.

11. There are _____ people in my family.

12. My zip code is _____.

13. The temperature today is _____ degrees.

On today's activity: (Circle one) — I did great! — I did OK. — I need help.

Date

Today's Challenge — **For each temperature, circle Hот,**
Comfortable, or Cold.

	90°F	HOT (circled) COMFORTABLE COLD		30°F	HOT COMFORTABLE COLD (circled)
1.	95°F	HOT COMFORTABLE COLD	2.	35°F	HOT COMFORTABLE COLD
3.	88°F	HOT COMFORTABLE COLD	4.	15°F	HOT COMFORTABLE COLD
5.	75°F	HOT COMFORTABLE COLD	6.	20°F	HOT COMFORTABLE COLD
7.	0°F	HOT COMFORTABLE COLD	8.	100°F	HOT COMFORTABLE COLD

On today's activity: (Circle one) — I did great! — I did OK. — I need help.

Name   **Date**

Today's Challenge

Fill in the grid with the numbers from the Math Jumble Activity poster.

Sums of 15 with 2 addends	Sums of 15 with more than 2 addends

Go Further

Create your own Math Jumble. Have a friend find and write five facts with sums of 15.

_____

_____

_____

_____

_____

Friend's name _____

On today's activity: (Circle one) I did great! I did OK. I need help.

Name _____

Date _____

Get Started — Rule out two. Write why.
Fill in the correct circle.

Troy picked 3 cards from a deck of cards. Which
addition sentence shows the sum of the cards?

(A) 1 + 2 + 3 = 6 _____   (B) 7 + 7 + 7 = 21 _____

(C) 7 + 8 + 6 = 21 _____   (D) 8 + 8 + 8 = 24 _____

Today's Challenge

1. Emmet picked 3 cards from a deck of cards.
   Which addition sentence shows the sum of the cards?

   (A) 10 + 10 + 10 = 30 _____ ☐

   (B) 4 + 9 + 10 = 23 _____ ☐

   (C) 4 + 9 + 9 = 22 _____ ☐

   (D) 4 + 4 + 4 = 12 _____ ☐

2. Emmet picked 4 cards from a deck of cards.
   Which addition sentence shows the sum of the cards?

   (A) 10 + 10 + 10 + 10 = 40 _____ ☐

   (B) 4 + 3 + 10 + 10 = 27 _____ ☐

   (C) 4 + 3 + 10 = 17 _____ ☐

   (D) 4 + 4 + 3 + 10 = 21 _____ ☐

Total points for Today's Challenge: _____

On today's activity: (Circle one) ◂ I did great! ◂ I did OK. ◂ I need help.

Name   Date   95

Today's Challenge

1. Look at the completed addition problems on this page.
Without adding, circle the incorrect sums.

Name: Maria

1.   7
  + 5
  12
	2. 13
	  + 5
	  19
		3. 23
		  + 15
		  38
			4. 37
			  + 15
			  43
				5. 45
				  + 35
				  80

6.   51
  + 17
  69
	7. 65
	  + 31
	  97
		8. 73
		  + 9
		  82
			9. 63
			  + 29
			  92
				10. 57
				  + 13
				  69

Copy and correct the addition problems that you circled.

2.   **3.**   **4.**   **5.**   **6.**

+ _____   + _____   + _____   + _____   + _____

Go Further

7. Look at the addition problem at the right.
Will the sum be an even number or an odd number?
How do you know?

                            99
                          + 95

_____

_____

On today's activity: (Circle one) I did great! I did OK. I need help.

Today's Challenge — Draw a line to match the correct letter.

1. the double of 9 is   **A.** 11

2. the double of 8 is   **B.** 7

3. half of 22 is   **C.** 5

4. the double of 7 is   **D.** 16

5. half of 10 is   **E.** 14

6. half of 6 is   **F.** 6

7. the double of 5 is   **G.** 9

8. half of 18 is   **H.** 10

9. half of 14 is   **I.** 3

10. half of 12 is   **J.** 18

Go Further — Circle the correct word.

11. When a number is **doubled**, the answer is **twice** / **half** as much.

12. When a number is **halved**, the answer is **twice** / **half** as much.

On today's activity: (Circle one) — I did great! — I did OK. — I need help.

Name   **Date**

Today's Challenge — For questions 1 and 2, circle **Yes** or **No**.

1. :

   a. Does it roll like a ball?   Yes   No

   b. Can it be stacked?   Yes   No

   c. Can it slide?   Yes   No

   d. Does it have only 1 round base?   Yes   No

   What is my name? _____

2. Clues:

   a. Can it be stacked?   Yes   No

   b. Does it have a square base?   Yes   No

   c. Can it slide?   Yes   No

   d. Does it roll?   Yes   No

   What is my name? _____

Go Further

3. Solve this riddle.

   Clues:

   · I can roll.

   · I can slide.

   · I can be stacked.

   · I have not one, but two round bases.

   · What is my name? _____

4. Write your own riddle for a friend to solve.

   Clues: _____

   _____

What is my name? _____   Friend's name _____

On today's activity: (Circle one) I did great! I did OK. I need help.

Date

Today's Challenge — Fill in the grid with the numbers from the Math Jumble Activity poster.

Sums of 16 with 2 addends	Sums of 16 with more than 2 addends

Go Further — Create your own Math Jumble. Have a friend find and write five facts with sums that equal 16.

_____

_____

_____

_____

_____

Friend's name _____

On today's activity: (Circle one) — I did great! — I did OK. — I need help.

Name

Date

Get Started — Rule out two. Write why. Fill in the correct circle.

When Carrie's tooth fell out, she put it under her pillow. The next morning she found 75¢. She put the three coins in her piggy bank. Which three coins did Carrie put in her bank?

A (coins) _____   **B** (coins) _____

C (coins) _____   **D** (coins) _____

Today's Challenge

1. Karim bought a juice box for 45¢. He paid for the juice box with three coins. Which three coins did Karim use to pay for the juice box?

   A (coins) _____ ☐

   B (coins) _____ ☐

   C (coins) _____ ☐

   D (coins) _____ ☐

2. The toll booth charge is 65¢. Which group of coins shows the correct amount?

   A (coins) _____ ☐

   B (coins) _____ ☐

   C (coins) _____ ☐

   D (coins) _____ ☐

Total points for Today's Challenge: _____

On today's activity: (Circle one) ⬤ I did great! ⬤ I did OK. ⬤ I need help.

2, 4, 6, 8 Pattern Puzzler

Today's Challenge Use markers or crayons to color the blocks shown. Then, complete each pattern by coloring the rest of the blocks for each pattern.

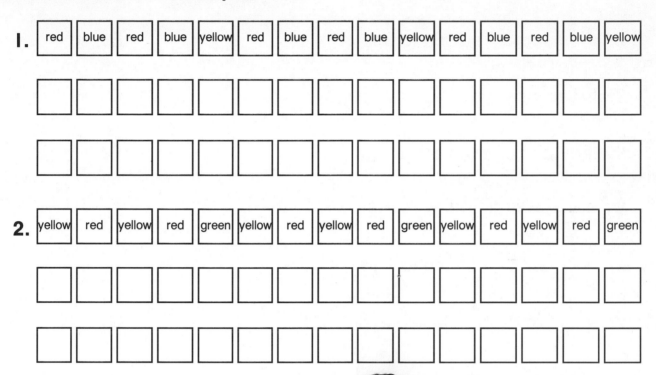

1. | red | blue | red | blue | yellow | red | blue | red | blue | yellow | red | blue | red | blue | yellow |

2. | yellow | red | yellow | red | green | yellow | red | yellow | red | green | yellow | red | yellow | red | green |

Go Further

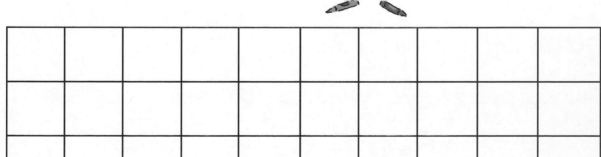

3. Color a pattern of your own. Use three different colors.

On today's activity: (Circle one) I did great! I did OK. I need help.

Name   **Date**   101

Today's Challenge Draw a line to match the correct letter.

1. the sum of 9 + 7 equals **A.** 8

2. the number you add to 3 to get 11 is **B.** 10

3. the number you double to get 8 is **C.** 14

4. the number you halve to get 6 is **D.** 1

5. the sum of 2 + 7 is **E.** 4

6. the number you add to 8 to get 10 is **F.** 6

7. the number you double to get 12 is **G.** 12

8. the number you add to 7 to get 8 is **H.** 2

9. the sum of 7 + 3 equals **I.** 16

10. the answer you get when you double 7 equals **J.** 9

Go Further Fill in the blanks.

11. _____ − 3 = 7   12. 11 − _____ = 8

13. _____ + 9 = _____

On today's activity: (Circle one) I did great! I did OK. I need help.

Date

Today's Challenge — Circle the correct amount to make $1.00.

Amount you have	Amount needed to make $1.00	Amount you have	Amount needed to make $1.00
60¢	10¢ 30¢ (40¢)	35¢	25¢ (65¢) 85¢
1. 50¢	10¢ 30¢ 50¢	2. 80¢	10¢ 20¢ 30¢
3. 20¢	50¢ 80¢ 90¢	4. 75¢	15¢ 25¢ 35¢
5. 45¢	15¢ 35¢ 55¢	6. 60¢	30¢ 40¢ 50¢
7. 35¢	65¢ 75¢ 85¢	8. 55¢	35¢ 45¢ 55¢

On today's activity: (Circle one) — I did great! — I did OK. — I need help.

Name

Date

Today's Challenge — Fill in the grid with the numbers from the Math Jumble Activity poster.

Sums of 17 with 2 addends	Sums of 17 with more than 2 addends

Go Further — Create your own Math Jumble. Have a friend find and write five facts with sums of 17.

_____

_____

_____

_____

_____

Friend's name _____

On today's activity: (Circle one) — I did great! — I did OK. — I need help.

104 Name

Date

Get Started — Rule out two. Write why. Fill in the correct circle.

What is the distance around the shape?

2 ft
2 ft 2 ft
2 ft

A 2 feet _____   **B** 4 feet _____

C 6 feet _____   **D** 8 feet _____

Today's Challenge

1. Nick has a square sandbox. What is the distance around the sandbox?

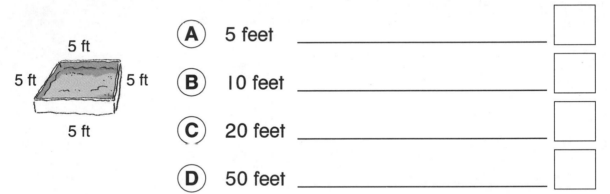

5 ft
5 ft   5 ft
5 ft

A 5 feet _____ ☐

B 10 feet _____ ☐

C 20 feet _____ ☐

D 50 feet _____ ☐

2. Tina has a vegetable garden. What is the distance around her garden?

8 ft
3 ft ▨ 3 ft
8 ft

A 8 feet _____ ☐

B 11 feet _____ ☐

C 16 feet _____ ☐

D 22 feet _____ ☐

Total points for Today's Challenge: _____

On today's activity: (Circle one) ◢ I did great! ◢ I did OK. ◢ I need help.

Name   **Date**

2, 4, 6, 8 Pattern Puzzler

Today's Challenge

1. Look at the numbers below. Circle the number pairs with a difference of 3.

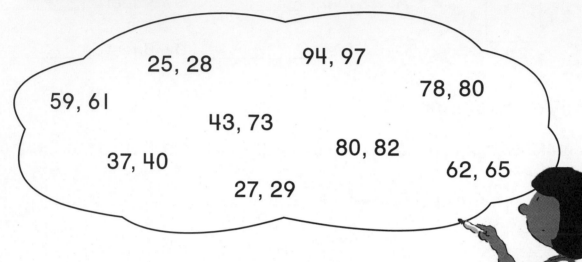

25, 28   94, 97

59, 61   78, 80

43, 73

37, 40   80, 82

27, 29   62, 65

2. Look at each pair of numbers that are not circled. Draw a square around all the pairs of numbers that have a difference of 2.

3. Which pair of numbers is left? _____

Go Further

4. Write six pairs of numbers that have a difference of 3. Use numbers between 50 and 100.

_____, _____   _____, _____   _____, _____

_____, _____   _____, _____   _____, _____

On today's activity: (Circle one) I did great! I did OK. I need help.

Name

Date

Today's Challenge — Draw a line to match the correct letter.

1. a problem that equals 20 + 1 is   **A.** 10 + 15

2. a problem that equals 5 + 7 is   **B.** 4 + 13

3. a problem that equals 9 + 10 is   **C.** 22 + 2

4. a problem that equals 11 + 11 is   **D.** 15 + 4

5. a problem that equals 7 + 3 is   **E.** 2 + 8

6. a problem that equals 11 + 7 is   **F.** 10 + 11

7. a problem that equals 10 + 14 is   **G.** 20 + 2

8. a problem that equals 12 + 13 is   **H.** 8 + 5

9. a problem that equals 10 + 7 is   **I.** 9 + 3

10. a problem that equals 6 + 7 is   **J.** 9 + 9

Go Further — Fill in the blanks with numbers you choose.

11. 14 + 10 = 24   _____ + _____ = 24

12. 9 + 4 = 13   _____ + _____ = 13

13. 10 + 5 = 15   _____ + _____ = 15

On today's activity: (Circle one) — I did great! — I did OK. — I need help.

Name   Date   **107**

Go Further — Follow the directions to cross out the times.

· Cross out all times that show ":00" minutes.

· Cross out all times that show 15 minutes after the hour.

· Cross out all times that show 30 minutes after the hour.

1. Which time is not crossed out? _____

2. What time do you get up in the morning? _____

3. What time do you get home after school? _____

On today's activity: (Circle one) I did great! I did OK. I need help.

Today's Challenge Fill in the grid with the numbers from the Math Jumble Activity poster.

Sums of 18 with 2 addends	Sums of 18 with more than 2 addends

Go Further Create your own Math Jumble. Have a friend find and write five facts with sums of 18.

_____

_____

_____

_____

_____

Friend's name _____

On today's activity: (Circle one) I did great! I did OK. I need help.

Name _____ **Date** _____

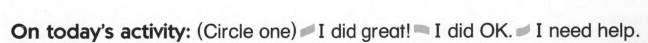

Get Started — Rule out two. Write why. Fill in the correct circle.

Susan puts 3 cookies each on 4 different plates. How many cookies is that in all?

(A) 3 + 3 = 6 _____   (B) 3 + 3 + 3 = 9 _____

(C) 3 + 3 + 3 + 3 = 12 _____   (D) 4 + 4 + 4 + 4 = 16 _____

Today's Challenge

1. There are 5 lunchboxes each on 3 tables. How many lunchboxes is that in all?

(A) 5 + 5 = 10 _____ ☐

(B) 5 + 5 + 5 = 15 _____ ☐

(C) 3 + 3 + 3 = 9 _____ ☐

(D) 3 + 3 = 6 _____ ☐

2. There are 3 pet cages in the science lab. There are 2 guinea pigs in each cage. How many guinea pigs is that in all?

(A) 2 + 2 + 2 = 6 _____ ☐

(B) 3 + 3 + 3 = 9 _____ ☐

(C) 2 + 3 = 5 _____ ☐

(D) 3 + 2 = 5 _____ ☐

Total points for Today's Challenge: _____

On today's activity: (Circle one) ⚊ I did great! ⚊ I did OK. ⚊ I need help.

110 **Name**

Date

2, 4, 6, 8 Pattern Puzzler

Today's Challenge Skip count by fives to complete each problem.

	1.		2.		3.		4.

1. 300
305
310
_____
320
325
_____

2. 350
355
_____
365
_____
_____
380

3. 800
805
_____
815
_____
_____
830

4. 725
730
_____
_____
_____
_____

Go Further

5. Circle the numbers that you say when you skip count by fives. Find the path from START to END.

START	435	453	455	460	465	452	535	551
	440	445	450	485	470	458	500	505
	450	435	456	451	475	456	495	510
	451	450	444	555	480	485	490	515 END

On today's activity: (Circle one) I did great! I did OK. I need help.

Name

Date

Today's Challenge — Choose answers from the box to fill in the blanks.

16	10	14	4	20
9	24	18	35	200

1. The number of wheels on 9 bicycles equals _____.

2. The number of sides in 3 triangles equals _____.

3. The number of legs on 1 turtle equals _____.

4. The number of tails on 10 dogs equals _____.

5. The number of pennies in 2 dollars equals _____.

6. The number of fingers on 7 hands equals _____.

7. The number of tires on 6 cars equals _____.

8. The number of paws on 5 cats equals _____.

9. The number of sleeves on 7 sweaters equals _____.

10. The number of ears on 8 dogs equals _____.

Go Further — Fill in the blanks.

11. $7 + 7 + 7 =$ _____

$7 \times 3 =$ _____

$3 \times 7 =$ _____

12. $4 + 4 + 4 + 4 + 4 =$ _____

$4 \times 5 =$ _____

$5 \times 4 =$ _____

On today's activity: (Circle one) — I did great! — I did OK. — I need help.

Date

Today's Challenge

$3 \times 2 = 6$ $2 + 2 + 2 = 6$

1. $6 \times \underline{} = 12$

2. $4 \times \underline{} = 24$

3. $10 + 10 + 10 = 30$ $3 \times \underline{} = 30$

4. $2 \times \underline{} = 18$

5. $9 \times \underline{} = 27$

6. $8 + 8 = 16$ $2 \times \underline{} = 16$

7. $7 + 7 + 7 + 7 = 28$ $4 \times \underline{} = 28$

8. $6 \times \underline{} = 54$

On today's activity: (Circle one) I did great! I did OK. I need help.

Name

Date

Today's Challenge ✐ Fill in the grid with the numbers from the Math Jumble Activity poster.

Sums of 19 with 2 addends	Sums of 19 with more than 2 addends

Go Further ✐ Create your own Math Jumble. Have a friend find and write five facts with sums of 19.

_____

_____

_____

_____

_____

Friend's name _____

On today's activity: (Circle one) ✐ I did great! ✐ I did OK. ✐ I need help.

Get Started ✎ Rule out two. Write why. Fill in the correct circle.

Which shape is made by putting together triangles?

A ⬡(trapezoid) _____   **B** ⬭ _____

C ◯ _____   **D** ⬭ _____

Today's Challenge

1. How many small triangles are needed to make the large shape?

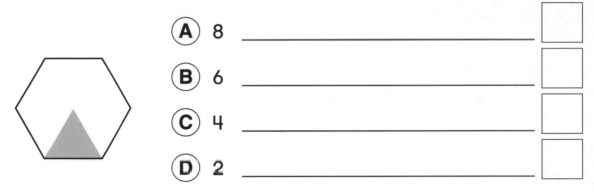

A 8 _____ ☐

B 6 _____ ☐

C 4 _____ ☐

D 2 _____ ☐

2. How many small triangles are needed to make the large shape?

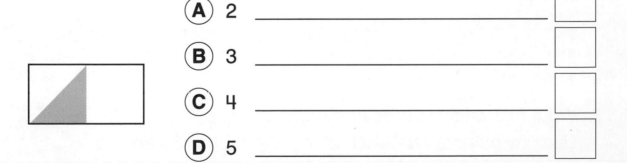

A 2 _____ ☐

B 3 _____ ☐

C 4 _____ ☐

D 5 _____ ☐

Total points for Today's Challenge: _____

On today's activity: (Circle one) ✎ I did great! ✎ I did OK. ✎ I need help.

Name   **Date**   115

Today's Challenge — **Circle all the problems that will have an odd sum. Then, write the sums for those problems.**

1. 23 + 45	2. 14 + 15	3. 53 + 9	4. 30 + 20	5. 39 + 11
6. 42 + 30	7. 35 + 18	8. 63 + 21	9. 25 + 52	10. 17 + 15
11. 33 + 55	12. 17 + 42	13. 54 + 20	14. 29 + 3	15. 48 + 12

16. What types of addends have an odd sum?

_____

_____

Go Further

17. Write four addition problems with odd sums.
Use any numbers between 20 and 50 for the addends.

+ _____   + _____   + _____   + _____

On today's activity: (Circle one) — I did great! — I did OK. — I need help.

Date

Today's Challenge — Choose numbers from the box to fill in the blanks.

20	58	140	72	40
70	75	47	97	68

1. 40 + 30 = _____

2. 60 + 80 = _____

3. 9 + 11 = _____

4. 10 + 37 = _____

5. 30 + 42 = _____

6. 20 + 20 = _____

7. 8 + 60 = _____

8. 25 + 50 = _____

9. 40 + 18 = _____

10. 80 + 17 = _____

Go Further — Fill in the blank.

11. _____ + 37 = 47

12. 9 + _____ = 20

13. 25 + _____ = 75

On today's activity: (Circle one) — I did great! — I did OK. — I need help.

Name _____

Date _____

Game Time

Today's Challenge What is the fewest number of coins needed to make the amount shown?

Amount	Fewest Coins Needed

14¢

___ 1 ___ 4

57¢

2 ___ 1 2

1.	6¢ 	2.	10¢ 

___ ___

3.	17¢ 	4.	75¢ 

___ ___

5.	38¢ 	6.	50¢ 

___ ___

7.	21¢ 	8.	40¢

___ ___

On today's activity: (Circle one) I did great! I did OK. I need help.

Date

Today's Challenge

1. Loop a string of coins that equals 31¢.

2. Loop a string of coins that equals 41¢.

3. Loop a string of coins that equals 17¢.

4. Loop a string of coins that equals 18¢.

5. Loop a string of coins that equals 45¢.

Go Further

6. What is the total amount of money shown in the Math Jumble? Write how you found your answer.

_____

_____

_____

_____

_____

_____

On today's activity: (Circle one) ⬛ I did great! ⬛ I did OK. ⬛ I need help.

Name **Date**

Get Started — Rule out two. Write why. Fill in the correct circle.

Jamie earns $2 each time he walks the family dogs. This week he walks the dogs twice. How much does he earn?

A $5 _____ **B** $2 _____

C $3 _____ **D** $4 _____

Today's Challenge

1. Mrs. Potter has 3 bags of potting soil. Each bag holds 10 pounds of soil. How many pounds of soil does Mrs. Potter have in all?

   A 3 pounds _____ ▢

   B 30 pounds _____ ▢

   C 10 pounds _____ ▢

   D 20 pounds _____ ▢

2. Jeb won 7 marbles every day for 3 days in a row. How many marbles did he win in all?

   A 10 _____ ▢

   B 7 _____ ▢

   C 3 _____ ▢

   D 21 _____ ▢

Total points for Today's Challenge: _____

On today's activity: (Circle one) ▬ I did great! ▬ I did OK. ▬ I need help.

120 Name

Date

Today's Challenge Fill in the missing numbers from the hundred chart. Look at the hundred chart in the back of your book if you need help.

1. | 23 |

2. | 47 |

3. | 35 |

4. | 69 |

5. | 80 |

Go Further Fill in the missing numbers without using the hundred chart.

6.
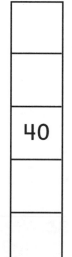
55

7.
40

8.
54

9.
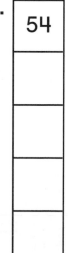
52

10.
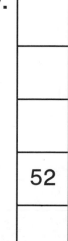
53

On today's activity: (Circle one) I did great! I did OK. I need help.

Name **Date**

Today's Challenge Draw a line to match the correct letter.

1. 100 + 5   A. 111

2. 700 + 4   B. 150

3. 100 + 50   C. 105

4. 100 + 10 + 1   D. 258

5. 600 + 10 + 3   E. 548

6. 200 + 60 + 3   F. 704

7. 100 + 60   G. 123

8. 200 + 50 + 8   H. 160

9. 100 + 20 + 3   I. 263

10. 500 + 40 + 8   J. 613

Go Further Write the three-digit number.

11. 20 + 100 + 5 = _____   12. 6 + 30 + 200 = _____

13. 700 + 3 + 10 = _____   14. 60 + 7 + 300 = _____

On today's activity: (Circle one) I did great! I did OK. I need help.

Date

Go Further — Follow the directions to cross out numbers.

121	363	575	100
801	183	238	151
488	105	343	177
153	737	111	709

- Cross out the numbers that have the digit 3 in the ones place.

- Cross out the numbers that have a 0 in the tens place.

- Cross out the numbers that have the same digit in the tens place and the ones place.

- Cross out the numbers that have the same digit in the hundreds place and the ones place.

1. Which number is left? _____

2. Write three ways to describe the number 125.

_____

_____

_____

On today's activity: (Circle one) — I did great! — I did OK. — I need help.

Name   **Date**

Today's Challenge Look for strings of repeating numbers to write an addition sentence. Then, rewrite each addition sentence as a multiplication fact.

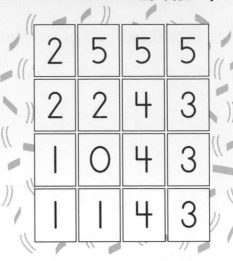

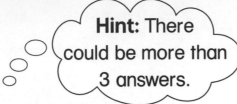

Hint: There could be more than 3 answers.

Addition sentences

_____ = _____

_____ = _____

_____ = _____

Multiplication facts

_____ × _____ = _____

_____ × _____ = _____

_____ × _____ = _____

Go Further Create your own Math Jumble. Use sets of repeating numbers from 0–5. Write two addition sentences using your numbers. Then, rewrite each addition sentence as a multiplication fact.

Addition sentences

_____ = _____

_____ = _____

Multiplication facts

_____ × _____ = _____

_____ × _____ = _____

On today's activity: (Circle one) I did great! I did OK. I need help.

Date

Get Started — Rule out two. Write why. Fill in the correct circle.

Billy needs a solid with a round bottom. Which solid does he select?

A _____   B _____

C _____   D _____

Today's Challenge

1. Rita wants to build a tower. Which solid should she put on the bottom?

A _____

B _____

C _____

D _____

2. Which solid is not the same as the others?

A _____

B _____

C _____

D _____

Total points for Today's Challenge: _____

On today's activity: (Circle one) ☞ I did great! ☞ I did OK. ☞ I need help.

Name   Date   125

Today's Challenge — Continue the pattern. Draw the squares, then write the number of squares.

1.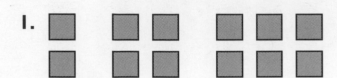

    2   4   6   _____   _____

2.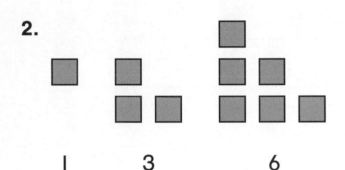

    1   3   6   _____   _____

Go Further

3. Look at the first pattern in problem 1. Describe the numbers you see.

_____

4. Look at the pattern in problem 2. How does the number of squares change from one group to the next?

_____

On today's activity: (Circle one) — I did great! — I did OK. — I need help.

Today's Challenge — Draw a line to match the correct letter.

1. $80 + \square = 100$
2. $25 + \square = 50$
3. $96 + \square = 100$
4. $17 + \square = 20$
5. $30 + \square = 100$
6. $50 + \square = 100$
7. $45 + \square = 50$
8. $10 + \square = 100$
9. $15 + \square = 30$
10. $10 + \square = 50$

A. 25
B. 3
C. 50
D. 20
E. 90
F. 40
G. 15
H. 5
I. 70
J. 4

Go Further — Fill in the blanks.

11. $1000 - \underline{\hspace{2cm}} = 900$

12. $1000 - \underline{\hspace{2cm}} = 800$

13. $1000 - \underline{\hspace{2cm}} = 700$

On today's activity: (Circle one) — I did great! — I did OK. — I need help.

Name

Date

Today's Challenge

Multiples of 2	Groups of 2		Addition	Multiplication
10			2+2+2+2+2	5 × 2
1. 6	_____	**2.**	2 + 2 + 2	___ × ___
3. 4	_____	**4.**	_____	2 × 2
5. _____		**6.**	_____	4 × 2
7. _____		**8.**	2+2+2+2+2+2	___ × ___

On today's activity: (Circle one) I did great! I did OK. I need help.

Name

Date

Today's Challenge ✏ Fill in the grid with the numbers from the Math Jumble Activity poster.

Sums greater than 20 but less than 50 with 2 addends	Sums greater than 20 but less than 50 with more than 2 addends

Go Further ✏ Create your own Math Jumble. Use numbers from 0 to 20. Have a friend write five facts with sums greater than 20 but less than 50.

_____

_____

_____

_____

_____

Friend's name _____

On today's activity: (Circle one) ✏ I did great! ✏ I did OK. ✏ I need help.

Name **Date** 129

Get Started — Rule out two. Write why. Fill in the correct circle.

Lola traced a lightning bolt pattern. Hogan did the same on another piece of paper. What did Hogan do to the pattern before he traced it?

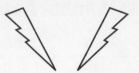

A He flipped it. _____

B He cut it. _____

C He slid it. _____

D He turned it. _____

Today's Challenge

1. How did Jane move the minute hand on the clock?

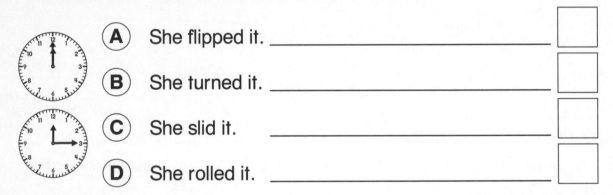

A She flipped it. _____

B She turned it. _____

C She slid it. _____

D She rolled it. _____

2. How did the face move from the top of the rectangle to the bottom of the rectangle?

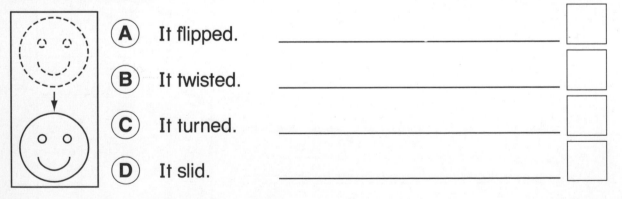

A It flipped. _____

B It twisted. _____

C It turned. _____

D It slid. _____

Total points for Today's Challenge: _____

On today's activity: (Circle one) ▰ I did great! ▰ I did OK. ▰ I need help.

130 Name

Date

2, 4, 6, 8 Pattern Puzzler

Today's Challenge

January						
Sun	Mon	Tue	Wed	Thu	Fri	Sat
	1	2	3	4	5	6
7	8	9	10	11	12	13
14	15	16	17	18	19	20
21	22	23	24	25	26	27
28	29	30	31			

1. Use the pattern yellow, yellow, green, yellow, yellow, orange to color the numbers 1, 2, 3, 4, 5, and 6. Then repeat the pattern of colors for the numbers 7, 8, 9, 10, 11 and 12. Continue until the whole calendar is complete.

2. Look at all the green numbers. Write them on the blanks. What pattern do you see?

   _____, _____, _____, _____, _____,

   _____

3. Find January 6 on the calendar. Write all the orange numbers on the blanks. What pattern do you see?

   _____, _____, _____, _____

   _____

Go Further

4. Color this calendar with a pattern you choose. How is your pattern different?

   _____

   _____

   _____

January						
Sun	Mon	Tue	Wed	Thu	Fri	Sat
	1	2	3	4	5	6
7	8	9	10	11	12	13
14	15	16	17	18	19	20
21	22	23	24	25	26	27
28	29	30	31			

On today's activity: (Circle one) I did great! I did OK. I need help.

Name _____ **Date** _____

Today's Challenge — Draw a line to match the correct letter.

1. 100 less than 600		**A.** 300
2. 300 more than 300		**B.** 650
3. 100 more than 200		**C.** 600
4. 400 more than 400		**D.** 950
5. 100 more than 0		**E.** 250
6. 100 less than 750		**F.** 700
7. 200 less than 550		**G.** 500
8. 500 more than 450		**H.** 100
9. 200 less than 900		**I.** 350
10. 500 less than 750		**J.** 800

Go Further — Fill in the blanks.

11. Skip count by fives.

185, 190, _____, 200, _____, _____, _____, 220

12. Skip count by tens.

120, 130, _____, _____, _____, 170, _____, _____, _____

On today's activity: (Circle one) — I did great! — I did OK. — I need help.

Date

Today's Challenge — For questions 1 and 2, circle Yes or No.

1. :

a. Do I have a point where some of my faces meet?
Yes   No

b. Do I have a triangular base?   Yes   No

c. Do I have 4 triangular faces?   Yes   No

d. Do I have more than 6 edges?   Yes   No

What is my name? _____

2. Clues:

a. Do I have 6 square faces?   Yes   No

b. Are all my faces the same shape and size?   Yes   No

c. Do I roll smoothly like a ball?   Yes   No

d. Can you stack me like a brick?   Yes   No

What is my name? _____

Go Further

3. Solve this riddle.

Clues:

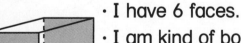

· I am a geometric solid.

· I have 6 faces.

· I am kind of boxy, but no one can call me a square.

· What is my name? _____

4. Write your own riddle for a friend to solve.

Clues: _____

_____

What is my name? _____   Friend's name _____

On today's activity: (Circle one) I did great!   I did OK.   I need help.

Name   Date

Math Jumble

Today's Challenge — Fill in the grid with the numbers from the Math Jumble Activity poster. Look for numbers with a difference greater than 10. Write the subtraction sentences.

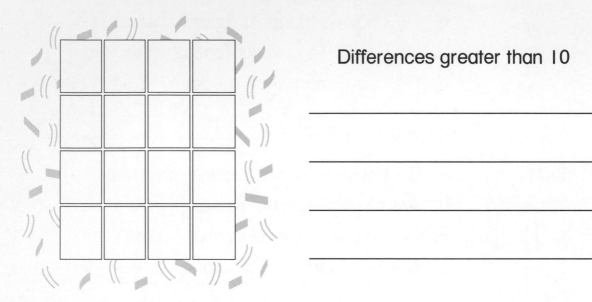

Differences greater than 10

_____

_____

_____

_____

Go Further — Create your own Math Jumble. Have a friend write five facts with differences greater than 10.

_____

_____

_____

_____

_____

Friend's name _____

On today's activity: (Circle one) — I did great! — I did OK. — I need help.

134 Name

Date

Get Started ✏ Rule out two. Write why. Fill in the correct circle.

There are 3 children at the art table. The teacher has 6 color markers. Which picture shows how many markers each child will get?

Ⓐ _____   Ⓑ _____

Ⓒ _____   Ⓓ _____

Today's Challenge

1. Four friends share a bag of marbles. There are 12 marbles. Which picture shows how many each friend will get?

   Ⓐ _____ □

   Ⓑ _____ □

   Ⓒ _____ □

   Ⓓ _____ □

2. The librarian has 18 books. Each shelf can hold 6 books. Which picture shows how many shelves are needed?

   Ⓐ _____ □

   Ⓑ _____ □

   Ⓒ _____ □

   Ⓓ _____ □

Total points for Today's Challenge: _____

On today's activity: (Circle one) ✏ I did great! ✏ I did OK. ✏ I need help.

Name _____   **Date** _____   135

2, 4, 6, 8 Pattern Puzzler

Today's Challenge — Find each product.

1.

$5 \times 2 = $ _____

$2 \times 5 = $ _____

2.

$4 \times 3 = $ _____

$3 \times 4 = $ _____

3.

$5 \times 4 = $ _____

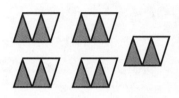

$4 \times 5 = $ _____

4. $1 \times 3 = $ _____

$3 \times 1 = $ _____

5. $3 \times 5 = $ _____

$5 \times 3 = $ _____

6. $4 \times 1 = $ _____

$1 \times 4 = $ _____

7. $2 \times 4 = $ _____

$4 \times 2 = $ _____

8. $5 \times 1 = $ _____

$1 \times 5 = $ _____

9. $3 \times 2 = $ _____

$2 \times 3 = $ _____

Go Further

10. If you know $2 \times 6 = 12$, then what is $6 \times 2 = $ _____?
Draw a picture to show 6×2.

On today's activity: (Circle one) — I did great! — I did OK. — I need help.

Name

Date

Today's Challenge — Choose answers from the box to fill in the blanks.

200	900	400	600	50
750	20	500	80	250

1. 400 + _____ = 1000

2. 500 + _____ = 1000

3. 800 + _____ = 1000

4. 250 + _____ = 500

5. 100 + _____ = 1000

6. 920 + _____ = 1000

7. 950 + _____ = 1000

8. 980 + _____ = 1000

9. 250 + _____ = 1000

10. 600 + _____ = 1000

Go Further — Fill in the blanks.

11. 1000 − _____ = 900   **12.** 1000 − _____ = 990

13. 1000 − _____ = 999

On today's activity: (Circle one) — I did great! — I did OK. — I need help.

Name _____   **Date** _____

Today's Challenge

Set	Fraction	Set	Fraction	Set	Fraction
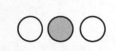	$\frac{1}{3}$		$\frac{2}{3}$		$\frac{3}{3}$ or a whole

1.	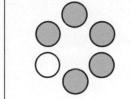	$\frac{}{3}$	**2.**	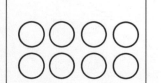	$\frac{}{4}$
3.	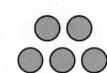	$\frac{}{6}$	**4.**		$\frac{}{5}$
5.	○○○○	$\frac{3}{4}$	**6.**	○○○○ ○○○○	whole
7.	○○○○ ○○○○	$\frac{5}{8}$	**8.**	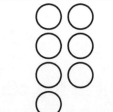	$\frac{5}{7}$

On today's activity: (Circle one) ⬤ I did great! ⬤ I did OK. ⬤ I need help.

Date

Today's Challenge ✏ Look for strings of repeating numbers to write an addition sentence. Then, rewrite each addition sentence as a multiplication fact.

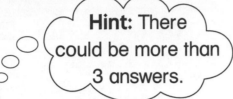

Hint: There could be more than 3 answers.

3	6	6	6
3	3	5	1
2	5	5	4
2	2	4	4

Addition sentences

_____ = _____

_____ = _____

_____ = _____

Multiplication facts

_____ × _____ = _____

_____ × _____ = _____

_____ × _____ = _____

Go Further ✏ Create your own Math Jumble. Use sets of repeating numbers from 2–6. Write two addition sentences using your numbers. Then, rewrite each addition sentence as a multiplication fact.

Addition sentences

_____ = _____

_____ = _____

Multiplication facts

_____ × _____ = _____

_____ × _____ = _____

On today's activity: (Circle one) ✏ I did great! ✏ I did OK. ✏ I need help.

Name

Date

Get Started ⟶ Rule out two. Write why. Fill in the correct circle.

Marvin buys milk at the school for 15¢. He pays for it with 1 quarter. What is the correct change?

Ⓐ _____   Ⓑ _____

Ⓒ _____   Ⓓ _____

Today's Challenge

1. The bus ride costs 60¢. Sherri pays with 3 quarters. What is the correct change?

Ⓐ _____

Ⓑ _____

Ⓒ _____

Ⓓ _____

2. The phone call costs 45¢. Marc pays with 2 quarters. What is the correct change?

Ⓐ _____

Ⓑ _____

Ⓒ _____

Ⓓ _____

Total points for Today's Challenge: _____

On today's activity: (Circle one) ⟶ I did great! ⟶ I did OK. ⟶ I need help.

Name   Date

2, 4, 6, 8 Pattern Puzzler

Today's Challenge

1. Look for patterns in the rows and columns. Then fill in the empty boxes.

2. Describe one pattern you see.

_____

_____

_____

_____

×	0	1	2	3	4	5
0	0	0	0	0	□	0
1	0	1	2	3	4	□
2	0	2	□	6	8	10
3	□	3	6	9	12	15
4	0	□	8	12	16	20
5	0	5	10	□	20	25

Go Further Use the table to fill in the blanks.

3. 3 × 1 = _____ **4.** 1 × 1 = _____ **5.** 5 × 1 = _____

3 × 2 = _____   1 × 2 = _____   5 × 2 = _____

3 × 3 = _____   1 × 3 = _____   5 × 3 = _____

3 × 4 = _____   1 × 4 = _____   5 × 4 = _____

3 × 5 = _____   1 × 5 = _____   5 × 5 = _____

On today's activity: (Circle one) I did great! I did OK. I need help.

Name   Date   141

Today's Challenge — Choose answers from the box to fill in the blanks.

66	50	33	10
4	55	42	60

1. I am halfway between 0 and 20. _____

2. I am a 2-digit number. My digits are the same. The sum of my digits is 12. _____

3. I am an even number. I am 10 less than 70. _____

4. I am a 2-digit number. My digits are the same. The sum of my digits is 10. _____

5. I am an even number. My ones digit is half of my tens digit. The sum of my digits is 6. _____

6. I am halfway between 0 and 100. _____

7. I am a 2-digit number. My digits are the same. The sum of my digits is 6. _____

8. I am an even number. If you double me, I am more than 5 but less than 10. _____

Go Further — Fill in the blank.

9. Write a number riddle. Give your riddle to a friend to solve.

_____

_____

On today's activity: (Circle one) — I did great! — I did OK. — I need help.

Date

Today's Challenge — Circle the sentence that is the same.

$$9 - 5 = 4 \quad \begin{array}{r} 9 \\ -4 \\ \hline 5 \end{array} \quad \boxed{\begin{array}{r} 9 \\ -5 \\ \hline 4 \end{array}} \quad \begin{array}{r} 5 \\ -4 \\ \hline 9 \end{array}$$

$$11 - 1 = 10 \quad \begin{array}{r} 11 \\ -10 \\ \hline 1 \end{array} \quad \begin{array}{r} 10 \\ -11 \\ \hline 1 \end{array} \quad \boxed{\begin{array}{r} 11 \\ -1 \\ \hline 10 \end{array}}$$

1. $8 - 6 = 2$	$\begin{array}{r} 8 \\ -2 \\ \hline 6 \end{array} \quad \begin{array}{r} 6 \\ -8 \\ \hline 2 \end{array} \quad \begin{array}{r} 8 \\ -6 \\ \hline 2 \end{array}$	**2.** $7 - 3 = 4$	$\begin{array}{r} 7 \\ -3 \\ \hline 4 \end{array} \quad \begin{array}{r} 7 \\ -4 \\ \hline 3 \end{array} \quad \begin{array}{r} 4 \\ -3 \\ \hline 7 \end{array}$
3. $9 - 3 = 6$	$\begin{array}{r} 9 \\ -6 \\ \hline 3 \end{array} \quad \begin{array}{r} 9 \\ -3 \\ \hline 6 \end{array} \quad \begin{array}{r} 6 \\ -3 \\ \hline 9 \end{array}$	**4.** $6 - 6 = 0$	$\begin{array}{r} 6 \\ -6 \\ \hline 6 \end{array} \quad \begin{array}{r} 6 \\ -0 \\ \hline 6 \end{array} \quad \begin{array}{r} 6 \\ -6 \\ \hline 0 \end{array}$
5. $12 - 10 = 2$	$\begin{array}{r} 12 \\ -2 \\ \hline 10 \end{array} \quad \begin{array}{r} 12 \\ -10 \\ \hline 2 \end{array} \quad \begin{array}{r} 10 \\ -2 \\ \hline 12 \end{array}$	**6.** $10 - 3 = 7$	$\begin{array}{r} 10 \\ -3 \\ \hline 7 \end{array} \quad \begin{array}{r} 3 \\ -10 \\ \hline 7 \end{array} \quad \begin{array}{r} 10 \\ -7 \\ \hline 3 \end{array}$
7. $15 - 5 = 10$	$\begin{array}{r} 15 \\ -10 \\ \hline 5 \end{array} \quad \begin{array}{r} 10 \\ -5 \\ \hline 15 \end{array} \quad \begin{array}{r} 15 \\ -5 \\ \hline 10 \end{array}$	**8.** $17 - 2 = 15$	$\begin{array}{r} 17 \\ -15 \\ \hline 2 \end{array} \quad \begin{array}{r} 15 \\ -2 \\ \hline 17 \end{array} \quad \begin{array}{r} 17 \\ -2 \\ \hline 15 \end{array}$

On today's activity: (Circle one) — I did great! — I did OK. — I need help.

Name **Date**

Math Jumble

Today's Challenge

1. Loop a string of coins that equals 95¢.

2. Loop a string of coins that equals 90¢.

3. Loop a string of coins that equals 60¢.

4. Loop a string of coins that equals 65¢.

5. Loop a string of coins that equals 35¢.

Go Further

6. What is the total amount of money shown in the Math Jumble? Write how you found your answer.

_____

_____

_____

_____

_____

_____

On today's activity: (Circle one) ⬭ I did great! ⬭ I did OK. ⬭ I need help.

Date

Get Started ☞ **Rule out two. Write why. Fill in the correct circle.**

Seven children come to music class late. The other 11 students are already sitting down. How many children are in music class?

(A) 4 _____   **(B)** 11 _____

(C) 7 _____   **(D)** 18 _____

Today's Challenge

1. Yesenia buys a computer game for $8 and a poster for $10. How much does she spend?

   (A) $2 _____ ☐

   (B) $10 _____ ☐

   (C) $8 _____ ☐

   (D) $18 _____ ☐

2. The temperature is now 75 degrees. Earlier it was 60 degrees. How much warmer is it now?

   (A) 75 degrees _____ ☐

   (B) 60 degrees _____ ☐

   (C) 15 degrees _____ ☐

   (D) 135 degrees _____ ☐

Total points for Today's Challenge: _____

On today's activity: (Circle one) ☞ I did great! ☞ I did OK. ☞ I need help.

Name _____   **Date** _____   145

2, 4, 6, 8 Pattern Puzzler

Today's Challenge — Fill in the missing numbers from the hundred chart. Look at the hundred chart in the back of your book if you need help.

1.
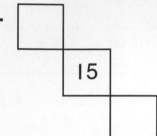
15

2.
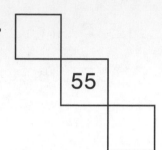
55

3.
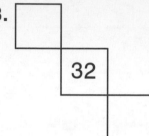
32

4.
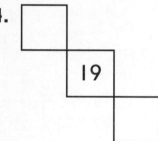
19

5.
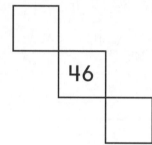
46

6.
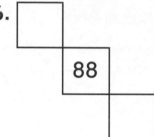
88

Go Further — Fill in the missing numbers without using the hundred chart.

7.
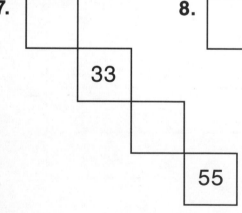
33
55

8.
45

9.
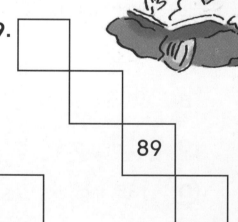
89

On today's activity: (Circle one) — I did great! — I did OK. — I need help.

Name

Date

Today's Challenge ⮞ Choose a number from the box to complete each sentence.

7	15	3	31	12
50	1	4	5	2

1. The number of stars on the American flag is _____.

2. The number of digits in the number 89 is _____.

3. The number of months with 31 days is _____.

4. The number of number of nickels in 1 quarter is _____.

5. The number of minutes in a quarter of an hour is _____.

6. The number of seasons in one year is _____.

7. The number of children in a set of triplets is _____.

8. The number of equators on Earth is _____.

9. The number of days in January is _____.

10. The number of months in 1 year is _____.

Go Further ⮞ Fill in the blank.

11. My house (or apartment) number is _____.

12. My telephone area code is _____.

13. At school, I am in grade _____.

On today's activity: (Circle one) ⮞ I did great! ⮞ I did OK. ⮞ I need help.

Name

Date

Today's Challenge — Circle the best choice.

less than I pound
about I pound
(more than I pound)

(less than I pound)
about I pound
more than I pound

less than I pound
(about I pound)
more than I pound

1.		less than I pound	2.		less than I pound
		about I pound			about I pound
		more than I pound			more than I pound
3.		less than I pound	4.		less than I pound
		about I pound			about I pound
		more than I pound			more than I pound
5.		less than I pound	6.		less than I pound
		about I pound			about I pound
		more than I pound			more than I pound
7.		less than I pound	8.		less than I pound
		about I pound			about I pound
		more than I pound			more than I pound

On today's activity: (Circle one) — I did great! — I did OK. — I need help.

Today's Challenge Fill in the grid with the numbers from the Math Jumble Activity poster.

Sums of 20 with 2 addends	Sums of 20 with more than 2 addends

Go Further Create your own Math Jumble. Use numbers from 0 to 20. Have a friend find and write five facts with sums of 20.

_____

_____

_____

_____

_____

Friend's name _____

On today's activity: (Circle one) I did great! I did OK. I need help.

Name **Date** 149

Get Started ✐ Rule out two. Write why. Fill in the correct circle.

Parker is cooking soup. Which tool should he use to measure the water needed?

(A) a ruler _____ **(B)** a scale _____

(C) a cup _____ **(D)** a clock _____

Today's Challenge

1. Carlos needs to time his speech. Which tool should he use to measure the time?

   (A) a ruler _____ ☐

   (B) a yardstick _____ ☐

   (C) a meter stick _____ ☐

   (D) a watch _____ ☐

2. Mrs. Price has a very heavy package. Which tool should she use to measure the weight?

   (A) a yardstick _____ ☐

   (B) a thermometer _____ ☐

   (C) a scale _____ ☐

   (D) a ruler _____ ☐

Total points for Today's Challenge: _____

On today's activity: (Circle one) ☞ I did great! ☞ I did OK. ☞ I need help.

150 **Name**

Date

Today's Challenge — Skip count by 20s for each problem.

1.	300	2.	600	3.	400	4.	700	5.	900
	320		_____		420		_____		_____
	_____		640		_____		_____		_____
	360		_____		_____		_____		_____
	_____		680		_____		_____		_____

Skip count by 20s. Write the missing numbers in the blanks.

6. 200, _____, 240, _____, _____

7. 500, _____, _____, 560, _____

8. 800, _____, _____, _____, _____

Go Further

6. Count by 20s from 440 to 660.

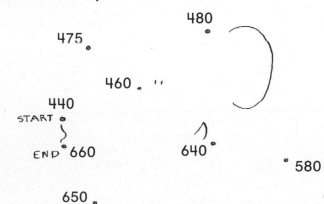
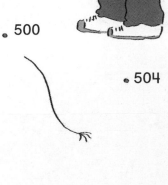

480
475
500
460
504
440
START
END 660
640
580 560
650
606
650
520
620 600 540

On today's activity: (Circle one) — I did great! — I did OK. — I need help.

Name   **Date**

Today's Challenge — Draw a line to match the correct letter.

1. the sum of 3 + 3 + 3   **A.** 0

2. the sum of 1 foot + 1 foot   **B.** 42

3. the first odd number after 80   **C.** 18

4. the number you add to 3 to get a sum of 8   **D.** 2 feet

5. the sum of 9 + 9   **E.** 9

6. the even number with 4 in the tens place   **F.** 81

7. the length of half a foot   **G.** 5

8. the length that equals 1 yard   **H.** 6 inches

9. the number I add to 7 to get a sum of 7   **I.** 11

10. the odd number between 9 and 13   **J.** 3 feet

Go Further — Fill in the blank.

11. $9 + _____ = 18$ 12. $_____ + 6 = 12$

13. $_____ + 7 = 14$ 14. $5 + _____ = 10$

15. $11 + _____ = 22$ 16. $_____ + 8 = 16$

On today's activity: (Circle one) — I did great! — I did OK. — I need help.

Date

Today's Challenge — Draw one of those shapes on your paper.

Go Further

1. Solve this riddle.

   Clues: · I have exactly 1 line of symmetry.

   · I have a curved shape with 1 point.

   · You all love me on Valentine's Day.

   · What is my name? _____

2. Write your own riddle for a friend to solve.

   Clues: _____

   _____

   What is my name? _____ Friend's name _____

On today's activity: (Circle one) — I did great! — I did OK. — I need help.

Today's Challenge — Fill in the grid with the numbers from the Math Jumble Activity poster.

Sums that are even numbers	Sums that are odd numbers

Go Further — Create your own Math Jumble. Have a friend write five addition sentences.

_____

_____

_____

_____

_____

Friend's name _____

On today's activity: (Circle one) — I did great! — I did OK. — I need help.

Date

Get Started ✏ **Rule out two.**
Write why. Fill in the correct circle.

The second graders voted on what to
have at their class picnic. Which food
item is the favorite?

Item	Student Votes
Hamburgers	7
Tacos	4
Pizzas	10
Fried Chicken	3

A hamburgers _____   **B** tacos _____

C pizzas _____   **D** fried chicken _____

Today's Challenge

1. How many second graders voted for hamburgers?

   A 3 _____ ☐

   B 4 _____ ☐

   C 10 _____ ☐

   D 7 _____ ☐

2. Which food item is the least favorite?

   A fried chicken _____ ☐

   B tacos _____ ☐

   C hamburgers _____ ☐

   D pizzas _____ ☐

Total points for Today's Challenge: _____

On today's activity: (Circle one) ▱ I did great! ▱ I did OK. ▱ I need help.

Name _____   **Date** _____   155

2, 4, 6, 8 Pattern Puzzler

Today's Challenge Fill in the missing numbers from the hundred chart. Look at the hundred chart in the back of your book if you need help.

1.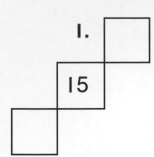
15

2.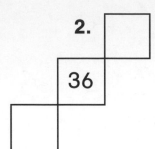
36

3.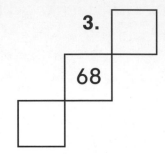
68

4.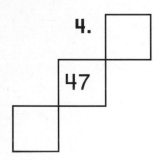
47

5.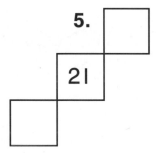
21

6.
89

Go Further Fill in the missing numbers without using the hundred chart.

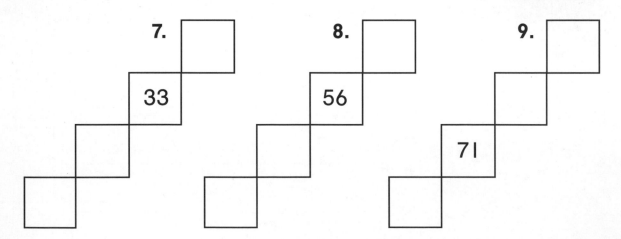

7. 33

8. 56

9. 71

On today's activity: (Circle one) I did great! I did OK. I need help.

Date

Today's Challenge — Draw a line to match the correct letter.

1. 20 fewer than 53 equals

2. twin coins worth a total of 20 cents

3. doubles that equal a sum of 10

4. 3 plus 8 equals

5. 2 coins worth a total of 50 cents

6. a subtraction problem with 100 and an answer that equals 10

7. 6 plus 6 equals

8. 2 coins where one is worth twice as much as the other

9. an addition problem with zero and an answer that equals 10

10. 0 plus 20 equals

A. $10 + 0$

B. 20

C. 12

D.

E.

F. $100 - 90$

G. $5 + 5$

H. 11

I. 33

J.

Go Further — Fill in the blanks.

11. $5 + 5 = 10$ is an addition sentence using doubles. Write two different addition sentences using doubles.

_____ + _____ = _____   _____ + _____ = _____

12. Show three coins that add up to 15¢.

On today's activity: (Circle one) I did great! I did OK. I need help.

Name

Date

Go Further — **Follow the directions to cross out numbers.**

9	30	12	17
25	15	8	5
5	7	0	4
3	20	10	2

- Cross out numbers in the subtraction fact family: $9 - 7 = 2$.

- Cross out the numbers that are 7 numbers away from 10 on a number line.

- Cross out the value of 3 nickels.

- Cross out the value of 3 nickels after spending 1 nickel.

- Cross out the value of 3 nickels after spending 2 nickels.

- Cross out numbers that are 4 numbers apart on a number line.

- Cross out numbers found by skip counting backwards by fives from 25.

Which number is not crossed out? _____

On today's activity: (Circle one) — I did great! — I did OK. — I need help.

Today's Challenge Fill in the grid with coin values from the Math Jumble Activity poster. Write 1¢, 5¢, 10¢ or 25¢ for each coin.

Coin amounts that equal $1

_____ = _____

_____ = _____

_____ = _____

_____ = _____

Go Further Create your own Math Jumble. Fill in the grid with the values of different coins. Have a friend write three addition sentences for different coins whose total value equals 100¢ or $1.00.

_____

_____

_____

_____

_____

Friend's name _____

On today's activity: (Circle one) I did great! I did OK. I need help.

Name _____ Date _____ 159

Get Started   Rule out two. Write why. Fill in the correct circle.

Which container holds the least amount of water?

 A _____   **B**  _____

C _____   **D** _____

Today's Challenge

1. Which container holds the least amount of water?

A    ☐

B    ☐

C  ☐

D ☐

2. Which container holds the most amount of water?

A   ☐

B    ☐

C    ☐

D   ☐

Total points for Today's Challenge: _____

On today's activity: (Circle one) I did great! I did OK. I need help.

Today's Challenge

1. Fill in the missing numbers in the chart to show 35¢ using pennies, nickels, dimes, and quarters.

Go Further

2. What number pattern do you see for the pennies in the chart?

_____

_____

_____

All the Different Ways to Make 35¢

Quarters	Dimes	Nickels	Pennies
1			
1			
	3		
	2		
	2		
		1	
	1		
		4	
	1	3	
			15
	1	1	
			25
		6	
			10
		4	
			20
		2	

On today's activity: (Circle one) ▬ I did great! ▬ I did OK. ▬ I need help.

Name

Date

Today's Challenge   Draw a line to match the correct letter.

1. Each song on the CD is 2 minutes long.
   How long will it take to play all 10 songs?   **A.** cylinder

2. 17 plus _____ equals 27   **B.** 20 minutes

3. the name of this solid is ⬭   **C.** 10

4. half the number of minutes in 60 minutes equals   **D.** 9

5. As a puppy, Maggie weighed 3 pounds. Now, she
   weighs 17 pounds. How much weight did she gain?   **E.** 14 pounds

6. 14 plus _____ equals 23   **F.** 30

7. half the number of pennies in 10 pennies equals   **G.**

8. half the number of inches in 12 inches equals   **H.**

9. a flat shape that is round   **I.** 5

10. a solid that is round all over   **J.** 6

Go Further   Loop the items to show half.

11.

12.

On today's activity: (Circle one) I did great!   I did OK.   I need help.

Date

Today's Challenge

 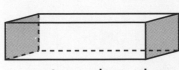

square pyramid   cube   cone   rectangular prism

1. 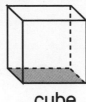	_____ pyramid	**2.** 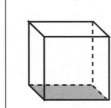	_____
3. 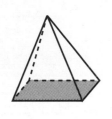	_____	**4.** 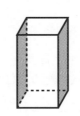	_____ prism
5. (draw solid)	cube	**6.** 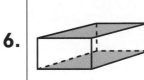	_____ prism
7. 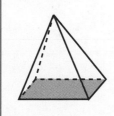	_____ pyramid	**8.**	_____

On today's activity: (Circle one) I did great! I did OK. I need help.

Name _____   **Date** _____   163

Today's Challenge ✏ Fill in the grid with the numbers from the Math Jumble Activity poster. Find four subtraction facts.

Subtraction facts

_____ – _____ = _____

_____ – _____ = _____

_____ – _____ = _____

_____ – _____ = _____

Go Further ✏ Create your own Math Jumble. Have a friend write five subtraction sentences.

_____

_____

_____

_____

_____

Friend's name _____

On today's activity: (Circle one) ✏ I did great! ✏ I did OK. ✏ I need help.

164 Name

Date

Get Started — Rule out two. Write why. Fill in the correct circle.

The lunchroom has 5 tables. Four children sit at each table. Select the multiplication sentence that shows how many children there are.

(A) 2 × 3 = 6 _____ **(B)** 5 × 5 = 25 _____

(C) 6 × 4 = 24 _____ **(D)** 5 × 4 = 20 _____

Today's Challenge

1. Diana has 3 boxes. There are 5 trading cards in each box. Select the multiplication sentence that shows how many trading cards there are.

   (A) 3 × 3 = 9 _____ ☐

   (B) 5 × 6 = 30 _____ ☐

   (C) 3 × 5 = 15 _____ ☐

   (D) 30 × 3 = 90 _____ ☐

2. Brandon 4 groups of matchbox cars. There are 10 cars in each group. Select the multiplication sentence that shows how many match box cars there are.

   (A) 2 × 3 = 6 _____ ☐

   (B) 5 × 5 = 25 _____ ☐

   (C) 4 × 10 = 40 _____ ☐

   (D) 5 × 3 = 15 _____ ☐

Total points for Today's Challenge: _____

On today's activity: (Circle one) ✏ I did great! ✏ I did OK. ✏ I need help.

Name **Date**

Today's Challenge — Complete the addition sentences and find the sums for each set of numbers.

1.

3	4
13	14

3 + 14 = _____

4 + 13 = _____

2.

33	34
43	44

33 + 44 = _____

34 + 43 = _____

3.

63	64
73	74

63 + 74 = _____

64 + _____ = _____

4.

83	84
93	94

83 + 94 = _____

84 + _____ = _____

5.

4	5
14	15

4 + 15 = _____

5 + _____ = _____

6.

42	43
52	53

42 + 53 = _____

43 + _____ = _____

Go Further — Find the 2 by 2 squares on the hundred chart for the sum. Fill in the numbers. Then complete the addition sentences.

7. SUM: 75

_____ + _____ = 75

_____ + _____ = 75

8. SUM: 119

_____ + _____ = 119

_____ + _____ = 119

9. SUM: 97

_____ + _____ = 97

_____ + _____ = 97

On today's activity: (Circle one) — I did great! — I did OK. — I need help.

Date

Today's Challenge — Draw a line to match the correct letter.

1. 30 minutes after 4:00   **A.** ![nickel]

2. double the number 20   **B.** ![clocks]

3. half an hour after 8:00   **C.** ![clocks]

4. 5 cents   **D.** 57

5. the number of states in the United States   **E.** 100

6. the number of socks in a pair   **F.** 26

7. the number of letters in the English alphabet   **G.** 50

8. 15 cents   **H.** 2

9. 2 more than 55   **I.** ![dime and quarter]

10. the number of years in a century   **J.** 40

Go Further

11. Draw 4 coins to show 8¢.

On today's activity: (Circle one) — I did great! — I did OK. — I need help.

Name   Date

Today's Challenge — Circle the correct measuring tool to answer the question.

	Question	Tool		Question	Tool
	What month is it?	(Calendar) Scale Yardstick		**How tall is the doorway?**	(Ruler) Watch Thermometer
1.	What is the temperature?	Ruler Watch Thermometer	2.	How tall am I?	Yardstick Watch Thermometer
3.	How tall is the bookshelf?	Yardstick Watch Thermometer	4.	How old are you?	Yardstick Watch Calendar
5.	How much does the book weigh?	Thermometer Clock Scale	6.	What time is it?	Thermometer Clock Scale
7.	How many days have passed by?	Yardstick Watch Calendar	8.	How much water is in the tub?	Yardstick Gallon Calendar

On today's activity: (Circle one) — I did great! — I did OK. — I need help.

Date

Today's Challenge
Fill in the grid with the numbers from the Math Jumble Activity poster. Find sums of 21.

Sums of 21 with 2 addends	Sums of 21 with more than 2 addends

Go Further
Create your own Math Jumble. Include at least five pairs of numbers with sums that equal 21. Have a friend write five facts with sums that equal 21.

_____

_____

_____

_____

_____

Friend's name _____

On today's activity: (Circle one) I did great! I did OK. I need help.

Name   **Date**

Get Started — Rule out two. Write why. Fill in the correct circle.

The hens laid 36 eggs today. If 12 eggs are put in each carton, how many cartons are needed?

(A) _____   (B) _____

(C) _____   (D) _____

Today's Challenge

1. Mina has 18 water bottles. If 6 bottles fit in one container, how many containers are needed?

   (A) _____ ☐

   (B) _____ ☐

   (C) _____ ☐

   (D) _____ ☐

2. Xavier has 15 CDs. If his CD carrier can hold 5 CDs, how many carriers are needed?

   (A) _____ ☐

   (B) _____ ☐

   (C) _____ ☐

   (D) _____ ☐

Total points for Today's Challenge: _____

On today's activity: (Circle one) I did great! I did OK. I need help.

170 Name

Date

2, 4, 6, 8 Pattern Puzzler

July						
Sun	Mon	Tue	Wed	Thu	Fri	Sat
	1	2	3	4	5	6
7	8	9	10	11	12	13
14	15	16	17	18	19	20
21	22	23	24	25	26	27
28	29	30	31			

Today's Challenge

1. Use the pattern blue, blue, orange, green, green, yellow to color the numbers 1, 2, 3, 4, 5, and 6. Then, repeat the pattern of colors for the numbers 7, 8, 9, 10, 11, and 12. Continue until the whole calendar is complete.

2. Look at all the yellow numbers. Write them on the blanks. What pattern do you see?

   6, _____, _____, _____, _____

   _____

3. Find July 4 on the calendar. Look at the diagonal downward to the left. Write all the green numbers on this diagonal on the blanks. What pattern do you see?

   4, _____, _____, _____, _____   _____

Go Further

4. Look at the calendar for July. Name two diagonals that have 5 numbers. List the numbers.

   _____

   _____

On today's activity: (Circle one) I did great! I did OK. I need help.

Name _____ **Date** _____

Today's Challenge — Choose answers from the box to fill in the blanks.

12	502	10	15 + 4	75
715	21	10 + 13	11	6

1. 700 + 10 + 5 equals _____.

2. The number of wheels on 4 tricycles is _____.

3. The number you double to get 12 is _____.

4. 25 + 50 equals _____.

5. The number of tails on 10 dogs is _____.

6. An addition that equals 20 + 3 is _____.

7. Half of the number 22 is _____.

8. An addition that equals 9 + 10 is _____.

9. 500 + 2 equals _____.

10. The number of days in 3 weeks is _____.

Go Further — Write the 3-digit number.

11. 50 + 300 + 8 = _____   **12.** 9 + 40 + 200 = _____

On today's activity: (Circle one) — I did great! — I did OK. — I need help.

Date

Today's Challenge — Complete the chart.

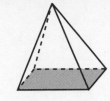
square pyramid

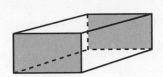
rectangular prism

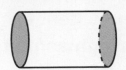
cylinder

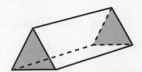
triangular prism

1.	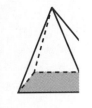	_____ pyramid	2. 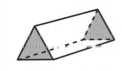	_____
3.	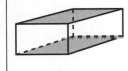	_____ prism	4. 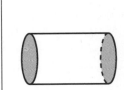	_____ prism
5.	(draw solid)	cylinder	6. 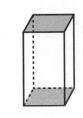	_____ prism
7.	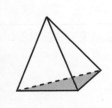	_____ pyramid	8. (draw solid)	square pyramid

On today's activity: (Circle one) — I did great! — I did OK. — I need help.

Name _____ **Date** _____ **173**

Today's Challenge
Look for strings of repeating numbers to write an addition sentence. Then, rewrite each addition sentence as a multiplication fact.

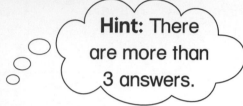

Hint: There are more than 3 answers.

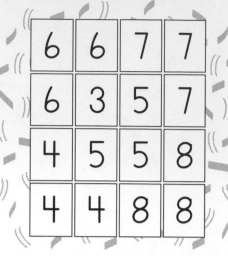

Addition sentences		Multiplication facts
_____ = _____		_____ × _____ = _____
_____ = _____		_____ × _____ = _____
_____ = _____		_____ × _____ = _____

Go Further
Create your own Math Jumble. Use sets of repeating numbers from 4–8. Then, rewrite each addition sentence as a multiplication fact.

Addition sentences		Multiplication facts
_____ = _____		_____ × _____ = _____
_____ = _____		_____ × _____ = _____

On today's activity: (Circle one) I did great! I did OK. I need help.

Get Started — Rule out two. Write why. Fill in the correct circle.

Which item below is a cube?

(A) _____   (B) _____

(C) _____   (D) _____

Today's Challenge

1. Which item below is a cylinder?

   (A) _____ ☐

   (B) _____ ☐

   (C) _____ ☐

   (D) _____ ☐

2. Which item below is a pyramid?

   (A) _____ ☐

   (B) _____ ☐

   (C) _____ ☐

   (D) _____ ☐

Total points for Today's Challenge: _____

On today's activity: (Circle one) — I did great! — I did OK. — I need help.

Name   Date   175

2, 4, 6, 8 *Pattern Puzzler*

Today's Challenge — Complete the addition sentences and find the sums for each set of numbers.

1.

8	9
18	19

8 + 19 = _____

9 + 18 = _____

2.

28	29
38	39

28 + 39 = _____

29 + 38 = _____

3.

68	69
78	79

68 + 79 = _____

69 + _____ = _____

4.

78	79
88	89

78 + 89 = _____

79 + _____ = _____

5.

6	7
16	17

6 + 17 = _____

7 + _____ = _____

6.

47	48
57	58

47 + 58 = _____

48 + _____ = _____

Go Further — Find the 2 by 2 squares on the hundred chart for the sum. Fill in the numbers. Then, complete the addition sentences.

7. SUM: 129

___ + ___ = ___

___ + ___ = ___

8. SUM: 165

___ + ___ = ___

___ + ___ = ___

9. SUM: 187

___ + ___ = ___

___ + ___ = ___

On today's activity: (Circle one) — I did great! — I did OK. — I need help.

Date

Today's Challenge — Draw a line to match the correct letter.

1. 500 more than 400 equals

2. $80 + \square = 100$

3. I am halfway between 0 and 12.

4. the number of months with 31 days is

5. $10 + \square = 100$

6. 100 less than 950

7. I am a 2-digit number. My digits are the same.
The sum of my digits is 8.

8. 100 less than 600

9. $40 + \square = 100$

10. the number of stars on the American flag

A. 20

B. 850

C. 7

D. 500

E. 6

F. 50

G. 900

H. 60

I. 44

J. 90

Go Further

11. Write a number riddle. Give your riddle to a friend to solve.

_____

_____

On today's activity: (Circle one) — I did great! — I did OK. — I need help.

Name   **Date**

Go Further — Follow the directions to cross out numbers.

12	8	21	10
17	20	13	14
24	5	25	9
30	6	19	27

- Cross out all numbers that can be divided evenly by 4.
- Cross out all numbers that can be divided evenly by 5.
- Cross out all numbers that can be divided evenly by 3.
- Cross out all numbers that can be divided evenly by 2.
- Cross out all numbers that can be divided by 6 and have 1 extra.

1. Which number is not crossed out?

_____

2. Write a story about 5 friends sharing 10 seashells.

_____

_____

_____

_____

On today's activity: (Circle one) ▬ I did great! ▬ I did OK. ▬ I need help.

Today's Challenge — Look for strings of repeating numbers to write an addition sentence. Then, rewrite each addition sentence as a multiplication fact.

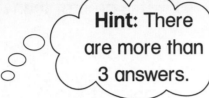

Hint: There are more than 3 answers.

Addition sentences

_____ = _____

_____ = _____

_____ = _____

Multiplication facts

_____ × _____ = _____

_____ × _____ = _____

_____ × _____ = _____

Go Further — Create your own Math Jumble. Use sets of repeating numbers from 5–9. Then rewrite each addition sentence as a multiplication fact.

Addition sentences

_____ = _____

_____ = _____

Multiplication facts

_____ × _____ = _____

_____ × _____ = _____

On today's activity: (Circle one) — I did great! — I did OK. — I need help.

Name _____ **Date** _____

Get Started ✏ Rule out two. Write why. Fill in the correct circle.

Which statement is **true** about the number 30?

(A) It is an odd number. _____   (B) It is an even number. _____

(C) It is greater than 50. _____   (D) It is greater than 100. _____

Today's Challenge

1. Which statement is **true** about the number 41?

(A) It is greater than 50. _____ ☐

(B) It is greater than 100. _____ ☐

(C) It is an odd number. _____ ☐

(D) It is an even number. _____ ☐

2. Which statement is **NOT true** about the number 101?

(A) It is not an even number. _____ ☐

(B) It is greater than 100. _____ ☐

(C) It is less than 100. _____ ☐

(D) It is an odd number. _____ ☐

Total points for Today's Challenge: _____

On today's activity: (Circle one) ✏ I did great! ✏ I did OK. ✏ I need help.

180 **Name**

Date

See how many of these questions about numbers you can answer. Fill in the circle for the correct answer.

1. Which number comes just before 75?

   (A) 65   (B) 70   (C) 74   (D) 76

2. Which group of numbers is in order from **least** to **greatest**?

   (A) 456, 455, 454, 453   (C) 145, 146, 137, 138

   (B) 292, 294, 296, 298   (D) 584, 582, 588, 583

3. In the number 846, what does the 4 mean?

   (A) 4 ones   (C) 4 hundreds

   (B) 4 tens   (D) 4 thousands

4. Which number is the same as four hundred five?

   (A) 4005   (B) 450   (C) 415   (D) 405

5. Which group of numbers has all **odd** numbers?

   (A) 6   8   12   (C) 5   10   11

   (B) 3   9   11   (D) 6   9   13

6. Circle all the numbers you would say if you were counting by twos.

   2   7   8   14   15   22   23

Name _____   Date _____

7. Write the number that is more than 62 and less than 64. _____

8. Fill in the missing number in this pattern.

110, 120, 130, 140, _____, 160, 170

9 Fill in the missing number in this pattern.

24, 23, 22, 21, _____, 19, 18

10. Count the flowers. How many are there? _____

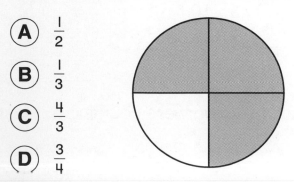

Now draw a loop around half the flowers.

How many flowers are in the loop? _____

11. Which picture shows 1 part out of 3 equal parts shaded?

(A)   (B)   (C)   (D)

12. Which fraction names the shaded part of the circle?

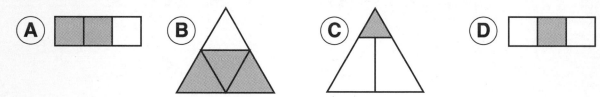

(A) $\frac{1}{2}$

(B) $\frac{1}{3}$

(C) $\frac{4}{3}$

(D) $\frac{3}{4}$

Math can be used every day to find the answers to many kinds of questions. See if you can find the answers to these questions.

1. You want to buy a pencil that costs 17 cents.
   Circle the coins you will need to pay for the pencil.

2. Katie ate 10 grapes. She was still hungry, so she ate 10 more.
   Katie wants to know how many grapes she ate altogether.

   Katie ate _____ grapes altogether.

3. Matt is reading a book that has 46 pages in it. So far he has read
   40 pages. Matt wants to know how many pages he has left to read.

   Mat has _____ pages left to read.

**These problems are all part of the same fact family.
Add or subtract.**

4.	5.	6.	7.
8 +6	14 −8	14 −6	8 +6

Add.

8.	9.
12 +13	15 +25

Name   Date

10. Fill in the circle for the correct answer.
Which number is 20 more than 56?

Ⓐ 36   Ⓑ 58   Ⓒ 76   Ⓓ 86

Subtract.

11.   15
    −4

12.   25
    −4

13.   25
    −14

Be careful, this one may be tricky!

14.   42
    −18

15. Choose the picture that matches this multiplication sentence.

$$4 \times 3 = 12$$

Ⓐ ☺☺ ☺☺ ☺☺ ☺☺ ☺☺ ☺☺

Ⓑ ♡♡♡ ♡♡♡ ♡♡♡ ♡♡♡

Ⓒ ✦✦✦ ✦✦✦

Ⓓ ⬭⬭ ⬭⬭⬭ ⬭⬭⬭⬭

16. There are 6 cookies in a package. How many cookies will
Dana and her friend get if they share the cookies equally?

They will each get _____ cookies.

17. Danny emptied his pockets and found 1 paper clip, 2 rocks, 1 quarter,
1 nickel, and 2 dimes. How much money did he have in his pockets?

Ⓐ 7¢   Ⓑ 28¢   Ⓒ 40¢   Ⓓ 50¢

Name

Date

**Everything has a shape! Some shapes have special names.
Draw a line from each of these shapes to its name.**

1. ▭   square

2. ◺   triangle

3. ▢   rectangle

4. Shapes come in all sizes. Circle the figure that is the same size and shape as the first one.

5. Circle the triangle that is the same size and shape as the first one.

6. Put an X on the shape that does not belong.

7. If Jayna wanted to walk all the way around the park in the picture, how far would she have to walk altogether?
Jayna would have to walk _____ miles.

2 miles

1 mile   1 mile

2 miles

8. Draw lines to match the hats to the word that tells how the hats were moved.

Flip

Slide

Name   **Date**

9. Draw a line on this shape to show how you could cut it into two parts that are exactly the same.

Here are some pictures of solid shapes. They all have special names too. Can you draw a line from each shape to its name?

10.   cylinder

11.   cube

12.   sphere

13.   cone

14. Blocks with different shapes can be used in different ways. Draw a circle around the shapes that can roll.

15. Draw a square around the shapes that can be stacked.

Date

Measurement

Measuring is a fun way to find out about the world you live in. See how much you already know by answering as many questions as you can. Fill in the circle for the correct answer.

1. Which tool would you use to measure your weight?

 A   **B**   **C**    **D**

2. Which could be the weight of a cat?

A 10 pounds   **C** 10 ounces

B 10 inches   **D** 10 tons

3. Which tool would you use to measure the length of your arm?

 A   **B**   **C**    **D**

4. If the temperature outside is 20°F, which would you want to do?

A Have a picnic.   **C** Build a snowman.

B Go swimming.   **D** Plant flowers.

5. Kari has these coins in her pocket. How much money does she have?

A 4 cents   **B** 17 cents   **C** 20 cents   **D** 22 cents

6. About how many paper clips long is the pencil?

A 2   **B** 4   **C** 6   **D** 8

Name

Date

Measurement

Which is which? Circle the best choice.

7. Which weighs about 1 pound?

a loaf of bread　　　　　a car　　　　　a dog

8. Which is about 1 foot long?

a loaf of bread　　　　　a car　　　　　an egg

9. Which is about 3 centimeters long?

a paper clip　　　　　a baseball bat　　　　　a jump rope

10. What time is shown on the clock?

A 6:00　　**B** 2:00　　**C** 9:30　　**D** 2:30

Circle the correct choice to answer each question about measuring.

11. How many pennies equal 1 nickel?　　2　　5　　10

12. How many inches equal 1 foot?　　12　　24　　36

13. How many quarts are in 1 gallon?　　2　　4　　16

14. How many minutes are in 1 hour?　　10　　60　　100

15. Three boys made a graph to show how many books they read last week.

Who read the most books? _____

How many books did he read? _____

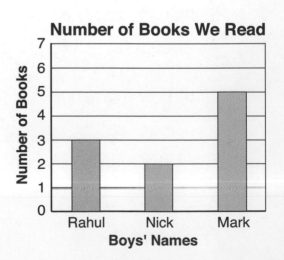

Number of Books We Read

Date

1. Draw the next shape for this pattern.

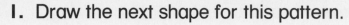

2. Draw the next shape for this pattern.

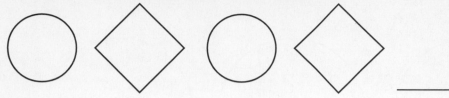

3. Draw the figure that comes next for this pattern.

4. Write the number that comes next in this pattern.

25, 30, 35, 40, 45, 50, _____

5. Write the number that comes next in this pattern.

22, 24, 26, 28, 30, 32, _____

6. Fill in the blanks in this pattern.

33, 32, 31, 30, 30, _____, _____, 27, 26

7. Circle the problem that will have an answer of 0.

23 + 7   18 − 18   18 − 9   18 − 17

Name _____   **Date** _____

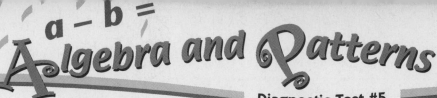

8. Look at the three groups below. Write the number 23 in the ring where it belongs.

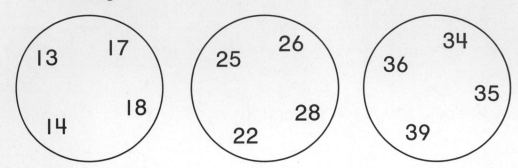

9. Look at the two groups below. Write the number 6 in the ring where it belongs.

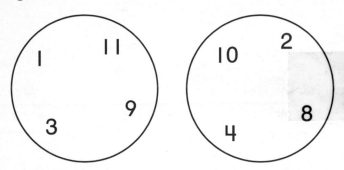

Write <, >, or = in the ◯.

10. 56 ◯ 49

11. 6 + 8 ◯ 8 + 6

12. 46 + 35 ◯ 35 + 46

13. 62 + 21 ◯ 21 + 37

Write the missing numbers.

14. 17 + _____ = 18

15. 42 + _____ = 42

16. _____ + 31 = 31

17. _____ + 49 = 50